Books should be returned on or before the
last date stamped below

HEADQUARTERS

2 1 APR 2005

1 5 JUN 2005

- 1 AUG 2005

20/9/05

- 1 OCT 2005

1 7 MAY 2006

- 9 JUN 2006

- 4 OCT 2006

2 7 NOV 2006

- 3 JAN 2007

- 6 FEB 2007

3 1 MAR 2007

2 8 APR 2007

2 6 MAY 2007

3 0 JUN 2007

- 3 SEP 2007

HEADQUARTERS

2 2 SEP 2008

2 4 OCT 2008

HEADQUARTERS

- 8 JUL 2009

1 2 SEP 2009

1 6 NOV 2009

- 1 DEC 2009

2 5 MAR 2010

- 5 APR 2010

2 2 MAY 2010

1 1 SEP 2010

1 1 JUL 2011

1 7 AUG 2011

2 9 SEP 2011

2 6 MAR 2012

risotto

risotto

with vegetables, seafood, meat and more

Maxine Clark

photography by Martin Brigdale

RYLAND
PETERS
& SMALL

LONDON NEW YORK

First published in Great Britain in 2005
by Ryland Peters & Small
20–21 Jockey's Fields
London WC1R 4BW
www.rylandpeters.com

10 9 8 7 6 5 4 3 2 1

ISBN 1 84172 811 X

A CIP record for this book is available
from the British Library.

Printed and bound in China

Dedication

I dedicate this book to my friend Pia Scavia,
a Milanese who is both inspirational and stoic
and doesn't mind using a stock cube.

Acknowledgements

My thanks go to all at RPS; Elsa and Alison for
encouraging me to write this book and Steve
for his patience at the studio, his good design
and enthusiastic risotto tasting. Martin has yet
again produced beautiful, natural-looking
photographs with a subject that is difficult to
control. Helen supplied us with evocative props
and backgrounds. My thanks to Bridget, for
producing some really beautiful risottos.
Belinda Spinney ably assisted me in the kitchen
and will probably never want to see rice in any
form again. Thanks too must go to Silvia
Brugiamolini at Esperya for dealing with my
wonderful rice order so efficiently – the rice
was a treat to use. I would like to add my
thanks to Antonietta Kelly at the Italian Trade
Commission for supplying information from The
Italian Association of Rice Producers. My
thanks also to Nowelle Valentino-Capezza for
her help with the translations.

Senior Designer Steve Painter
Commissioning Editor
      Elsa Petersen-Schepelern
Art Director Gabriella Le Grazie
Publishing Director Alison Starling

Food Stylists Maxine Clark,
      Bridget Sargeson
Prop Stylist Helen Trent
Indexer Hilary Bird

Notes

- All spoon measurements are level unless otherwise stated.
- All herbs are fresh, unless specified otherwise.
- Ingredients in this book are available from larger supermarkets, specialist greengrocers and delicatessens. See page 142 for mail order sources.
- Eggs are medium unless otherwise specified. Uncooked or partly cooked eggs should not be served to the very old, the frail, young children, pregnant women or those with compromised immune systems.

contents

calming, sensuous, satisfying …

Making a risotto is one of the most calming, sensuous, satisfying cooking experiences I know. Make it in a hurry at your peril – this is a dish to be made after a hard day, while you're winding down with a glass of wine. Though the cooking process takes only about 30 minutes from beginning to end, it's best to do all the preparation before you start cooking the rice. Have the stock ready and keep it hot over very gentle heat while you make the risotto.

There are no sudden movements when risotto-making. The butter is melted very gently, the chopped vegetables are added and slowly cooked in their own juices until soft. The rice is added and pan-toasted until it smells vaguely nutty, then the wine is splashed in 'with a sigh'. The stock is gently ladled in, sighing again each time. Then the rice is stirred languorously to encourage the starch to leave the outside of the grains and thicken the sauce. The bubbles in the liquid move and burst slowly. The rice should always look voluptuous and never be allowed to dry out.

Almost anything can be cooked into a risotto – and it can be added right at the beginning before the rice if it should be cooked for longer than 12–20 minutes, or it can be stirred in at the end. Traditional methods of cooking vegetable risottos like asparagus involve adding the vegetables early so they disintegrate into the risotto, cooking and sealing the flavour into the creaminess of the dish. It is now more fashionable to stir in precooked vegetables to give a contrast between mild creamy rice and the added ingredient. But it is all a matter of taste. People get very wound up about whether a risotto should be soupy and very firm – others like it creamy and thick. Ignore what people say and cook it as you like it. Just don't overcook it to a mushy porridge – that is unkind to the rice as well as your taste buds.

ingredients and utensils

The cultivation of rice in Italy

The cultivation of rice is as ancient as the making of wine and olive oil, thus providing a staple on which people could survive. Italian rice has its genetic roots in the original species *Oryza sativa*, a member of the Gramineae or grass family, the *japonica* subspecies of which is said to have been brought to Europe through Arab expansion into the Mediterranean basin. It was probably known before this time, arriving via the busy trade routes with the Middle and Far East, where it had been cultivated for thousands of years. The *japonica* has a higher starch content than the other most important subspecies, *indica*. Italian rice cultivation is concentrated in the Po Valley in northern Italy (Piedmont and Lombardy), but it is also grown around Venice, in Emilia Romagna, Sardinia and a little in Tuscany and Calabria. Rice production soared in the latter part of the nineteenth century after the development of manageable irrigation in Vercelli in Piedmont coupled with the invention of bigger and better rice-milling machinery. Vercelli is now the epicentre of rice-growing in Europe and has a rice stock exchange, the Borsa del Riso. New varieties have been developed since the singular variety simply called *nostrale* was consumed across Italy for over 400 years from the fifteenth century, so that more than 50 varieties are now available. Although rice is no longer considered a staple or 'food of the poor', the average Italian still eats about 5 kilograms of rice per year, in the late 19th century, it was more than double that amount. Rice is planted in flooded fields in March, and takes 180 days to grow and finally ripen for harvest in October. Until 40 years ago, rice was still picked by hand, but now it is gathered by huge combine harvesters. It is reaped, threshed and dried, then sold for milling and distribution. The milling process removes any dust, immature grains and the outer husk. Then it is polished to remove a second 'sheath' and the broken grains removed from the whole ones. Some rice is still polished *all'antica* (in the old way) using stone pestles (*lavorato con pestelli*) that give the grain a rougher, more rustic appearance and a little more fibre.

Which Italian risotto rice is best?

There are three varieties readily available around the world: arborio, carnaroli and vialone nano – these are the best for making risotto. In general, I like to use carnaroli or vialone nano, with arborio being last though not least favourite. Arborio is the most popular variety of short grain risotto rice. It has a slightly higher 'stickiness' or starch rating which makes it good for timbales and very creamy risottos. Personally, I think that arborio can become too mushy too quickly, whereas carnaroli has wonderful absorption, releases enough starch to make the risotto creamy and not sticky, while the grains still remain firm – *al dente*. Carnaroli is the rice preferred by most Italian cooks. Vialone nano has a shorter grain, a good absorption when cooked and is another rice with low stickiness or starch. This is preferred in the Veneto and Mantova in Lombardy for traditional recipes that require a looser risotto with a firm grain. Other newer risotto varieties available in Italy are baldo and Roma, which are both high in starch and make very creamy risottos and good timbales.

There are many other types of rice, but not all are suitable for risotto-making.

Italian rice is divided into four group classifications by law: *originario* or *comune, semifino, fino* and *superfino*. This doesn't denote quality or 'cookability', but length, appearance and shape. Every packet should display the group and variety.

Can I use another rice instead of Italian risotto rice?

No. Rice suitable for making risotto has a 'pearl' in the centre of the grain. On inspection, you will clearly see that the centre is whiter than the surrounding edges. This opaque central zone is made up of a farinaceous starch that is different from the starch on the outside of the grain. During cooking the outside starch dissolves into the liquid when the rice is stirred or beaten, while the interior starch absorbs liquid and swells. *Indica* rices such as basmati, Thai jasmine and American long grain rice do not have this 'pearl' in the centre. Therefore, Italian risotto rice is the only rice with the right make-up to absorb a large amount of liquid, release starch as it is stirred to make a creamy sauce, yet retain the shape and firmness of the grain without disintegrating and becoming gluey. Risotto is never gluey – it is always moist and creamy.

How do I store rice?

Rice absorbs moisture and odours, so store it like wine in a cool, dry, airy place. I keep it in an airtight storage jar well away from the oven or stove-top. If you like the look of the packaging, put the whole thing into a glass preserving jar with a rubber seal, close and admire!

What does *al dente* mean?

This means that the centre of the grain of rice is still firm to the bite, but cooked and definitely not mushy. It still has some delicate resistance. Some (especially the Venetians) say that the rice should still be a little gritty or chalky in the centre, but this is personal and I do not like it like that. You can take this *al dente* business too far.

Butter – salted or unsalted?

Always unsalted – it gives a purer, sweeter flavour.

Real stock or cubes?

Ideally, real stock is better, as it is the heart of the risotto, but it must not be too strong. Realistically, most Italians would use a stock cube to make an everyday risotto, but they are lucky to have quite a

choice available and I think that their cubes are of a better quality than those available elsewhere. *Gusto Classico* is a good all-round flavour – it is light and suitable for meat or poultry dishes.

How much stock?

As much as the rice will take. Always have more stock ready than the recipe states – you never know how much that particular rice will absorb on that particular day. It depends on and the type of pan you use and how fast the rice is bubbling (too fast and the stock evaporates instead of being absorbed into the rice).

Which pan to use?

A medium to large shallow pan (but not like a frying pan) with a heavy base. Enamelled cast iron or heavy stainless steel with a sandwiched base are good. I have a deep, heavy-gauge aluminium sauté pan that is perfect for risotto-making. A thin, flimsy pan is not suitable – the rice will stick and burn and you will not be able to control the simmer. Use too wide or shallow a pan, and the stock will evaporate too quickly and concentrate its flavour too much into the rice. Too deep and the rice will take ages to cook – it will stew and become mushy. All in all, a heavy saucepan that is not too deep is the answer. Make sure it is big enough to enable you to stir comfortably and for the rice to swell.

Parmigiano Reggiano or bust!

You do not have to use real Parmigiano Reggiano for risotto all the time. Parmigiano is a hard *grana* cheese with a D.O.P. status (*Denominazione d'Origine Protetta*), which promotes the authenticity and artisan characteristics of certain food and agricultural products – this one can come only from the provinces of Modena, Reggio Emilia, Parma and part of Bologna and Mantua, and is made in a particular way. Grana Padano D.O.P. is a less expensive *grana* cheese made in the Po Valley, and is perfectly acceptable to stir into a risotto. Fresh *grana* should smell sweet and nutty – never use the stuff found in the round cardboard canister. Extra cheese is not generally served with a fish or seafood risotto, the one exception being black squid ink risotto.

To shave or not to shave ...

Personally, I don't like shaved Parmesan on a risotto – it sticks to the rice like a soggy blanket and the heat makes it floppy and greasy. I prefer the cheese finely grated almost to a powder, so it will melt smoothly into the risotto.

the basics

white risotto step by step

risotto in bianco

This is the method for a basic, unflavoured risotto without cheese. The method always remains the same, but the ingredients change slightly. Sometimes, instead of plain onion, a *soffritto* – a finely chopped mixture of onion, carrot and celery – can delicately flavour the base of a risotto. Cubed pancetta is sometimes added at this stage, but must not be allowed to colour or it will become tough. Although the stated amount of stock is correct, I like to top it up to 2 litres just in case the rice becomes too thick (you could use hot water instead). The important thing is not to rush making a risotto – treat it with love and respect and you will achieve perfect results.

Note This recipe gives 4 very generous main course servings or 6 smaller servings. Allow 100 g rice per person for a generous serving, but less if adding a lot of meat or vegetables.

about 1.5 litres hot Light Chicken Stock (page 16) or Vegetable Stock (page 15)

125 g unsalted butter

1 onion, finely chopped

500 g risotto rice

150 ml dry white wine (optional)

sea salt and freshly ground black pepper

Serves 4–6

white risotto step by step

risotto in bianco

1

Put the stock in a saucepan and keep at a gentle simmer. Melt half the butter in a large, heavy saucepan and add the onion. Cook gently for 10 minutes until soft, golden and translucent but not browned.

2

Add the rice and stir until well coated with the butter and heated through (this is called the *tostatura* and the rice should start to crackle slightly).

3

Pour in the wine, if using – you should hear a 'sigh' (*sospiro*) as it is added. Boil hard until it has reduced and almost disappeared. This will remove the taste of raw alcohol.

4

Begin adding the stock, a large ladle at a time, stirring gently until each ladle has been almost absorbed into the rice. The risotto should be kept at a bare simmer throughout cooking, so don't let the rice dry out – add more stock as necessary. Continue until the rice is tender and creamy, but the grains still firm. This should take 15–20 minutes, depending on the type of rice used – check the packet instructions.

5

Taste and season well with salt and pepper and beat in the remaining butter (this process of beating is called *mantecare*).

Note Sometimes, according to the recipe, grated Parmesan cheese is beaten in with the butter at this stage.

6

Cover and let rest for a couple of minutes so the risotto can relax and any cheese will melt, then serve immediately. Venetians believe risotto should be served *al onda* (like a wave), referring to its liquid texture – so you may like to add a little more hot stock just before you serve to loosen it, but don't let the risotto wait too long or the rice will turn mushy.

Too many vegetable stocks are insipid or taste of a single ingredient. This stock is extravagant in its use of vegetables, but will have very good flavour. Stock gives a risotto body and depth of flavour, but shouldn't dominate the dish. Strong root vegetables such as turnips and parsnips are not good additions, and neither are potatoes or cabbage. Although you should always use the best and freshest ingredients, bits and pieces lurking in the refrigerator vegetable drawer can be used. Remember to wash everything first or you will end up with gritty stock. If you want a stronger stock, just strain, then boil hard to reduce it.

vegetable stock
brodo vegetale

1 large onion, quartered

2 large carrots, quartered

1 small bunch of celery, coarsely chopped (including leaves)

2 leeks, white parts only, halved lengthways, rinsed and halved again

4 courgettes, thickly sliced

2 tomatoes, halved around the middle and seeds squeezed out

1 fennel bulb, quartered

1 cos lettuce heart, coarsely chopped

3 garlic cloves

1 dried red chilli

4 fresh bay leaves

a handful of parsley stalks, crushed

½ lemon, sliced

6 black peppercorns

salt, to taste

Makes 2–3 litres

Put all the ingredients in a large stockpot. Add water to cover, about 4 litres, and bring to the boil. As soon as it boils, reduce the heat and simmer for 15 minutes. Stir the stock and skim off the foam, then cook at the barest simmer for 1 hour, skimming often.

Remove from the heat and strain the stock into a bowl through a colander lined with muslin. Discard the contents of the colander after they have cooled. Cool the stock and refrigerate for several hours.

At this stage you can reboil the stock to concentrate it, or cover and chill in the refrigerator or freeze until needed. The stock will keep in the refrigerator for 3 days or frozen for up to 6 months.

light chicken stock
brodo di pollo

Although Italians are not shy of using stock cubes (*dadi di brodo*), a good stock is worth making and can add real depth of flavour to a risotto. It is important not to make the stock too concentrated or dark in colour – it mustn't mask the true flavours in the risotto. You can make the stock using a whole chicken instead of chicken wings if you like, but I think this is sometimes a waste and chicken wings are flavoursome and give a good jellied stock.

1.5 kg chicken wings

2 carrots, coarsely chopped

2 onions, coarsely chopped

1 whole small bunch of celery including any leaves, trimmed, coarsely chopped, then washed

1 large fresh bouquet garni (bay leaves, thyme, rosemary and parsley stalks, tied up with kitchen string)

a few black peppercorns

Makes 2–3 litres

Cut the chicken wings into pieces through their joints. Put these into a large stockpot with the carrots, onions, celery, bouquet garni and peppercorns. Add water to cover, about 4 litres, and bring to the boil. As soon as it boils, reduce the heat to a simmer, stir and skim, then continue to cook at the barest simmer for 3 hours, skimming often. Remove from the heat and strain the stock into a bowl through a colander lined with muslin.

When cool, discard the contents of the colander. Cool the stock and refrigerate for several hours. Remove from the refrigerator and lift off any fat that has set on top of the jellied stock. At this stage you can reboil the stock to concentrate it, or cover and refrigerate or freeze until needed. This stock will keep in the refrigerator for about 3–4 days or in the freezer for up to 6 months.

game stock
brodo di cacciagione

For a rich, full flavour, the carcasses are browned before simmering with the vegetables. To make it darker, add the onion skins with the vegetables. If making duck stock, render the skin over medium heat to release the fat, then add the carcasses and brown them all over. Duck fat contains lots of flavour – skim the fat off later when the stock has cooled and set.

50 g unsalted butter

1 kg carcasses (plus any cleaned giblets, except the liver) of feathered game, chopped

1 onion, chopped

1 leek, split, washed and chopped

1 carrot, chopped

2 celery stalks, chopped

a few fresh parsley stalks, lightly crushed

6 black peppercorns

a pinch of salt

Makes about 2 litres

Melt the butter in a large stockpot. When foaming, add the carcasses and fry over low heat until light brown and on no account burnt. Add all the remaining ingredients and stir well. Add water to cover, about 3 litres, and bring to the boil. As soon as it boils, reduce the heat to a simmer, stir and skim the surface, then continue to cook at the barest simmer for 2 hours, skimming often. Remove from the heat and strain the stock into a bowl through a colander lined with muslin.

When cool, discard the contents of the colander. Cool the stock and refrigerate for several hours. Remove from the refrigerator and lift off any fat that has set on top of the jellied stock. At this stage you can reboil the stock to concentrate it, or cover and refrigerate or freeze until needed. This stock will keep in the refrigerator for about 3–4 days or in the freezer for up to 6 months.

I like to use a light stock for making risotto, therefore I do not brown the meat, bones or vegetables before simmering. My stock has body and is well flavoured. However, if you prefer a richer stock, brown the bones in a hot oven and, while they are browning, fry the meat and vegetables in the stockpot until they are a good red-brown, but do not let them over-brown or they will give the stock a bitter taste. If you don't have access to bones (these do give a great deal of body to the stock), add the same weight of beef or veal with good amounts of connective tissue – such as you find in cheap, tough cuts.

beef or veal stock

brodo di manzo o vitello

800 g shin of beef or veal or brisket
500 g beef or veal bones
1 onion, coarsely chopped
2 carrots, coarsely chopped
2 leeks, split, washed and chopped
2 celery stalks, coarsely chopped
a few parsley stalks, lightly crushed
2 bay leaves
6 whole black peppercorns
a pinch of salt

Makes 2–3 litres

Put all the ingredients in a large stockpot. Add enough water to cover, about 4 litres, and bring to the boil. As soon as it boils, reduce the heat to simmering, stir and skim the surface, then continue to cook at the barest simmer for 3 hours, skimming often.

Remove from the heat and strain the stock into a bowl through a colander lined with muslin. Discard the contents of the colander, after they have cooled. Cool the stock, then refrigerate for several hours. Remove from the refrigerator and lift off any fat that has set on top of the jellied stock.

At this stage you can reboil the stock to concentrate it, or cover and refrigerate or freeze until needed. This stock will keep in the refrigerator for about 3–4 days or in the freezer for up to 6 months.

Variation Game Stock with Wild Boar or Venison
When a recipe calls for game stock, make the recipe above, using wild boar or venison meat and bones (or veal bones), or use beef stock instead.

fish stock

brodo di pesce

Use trimmings (skin) and bones left from filleting white fish such as sole, plaice, cod or haddock. Oily fish like salmon, sardines and mackerel should be avoided (they are too strong in flavour). I simmer the vegetables before adding the fish trimmings and bones. This will extract more flavour, because if the fish is cooked longer than 20 minutes, the stock will be bitter.

1 leek, split, washed and chopped

2 celery stalks, coarsely chopped

1 carrot, coarsely chopped

a few parsley stalks, lightly crushed

2 fresh bay leaves

3 thick lemon slices

4 black peppercorns and a good pinch of salt

100 ml dry white wine

1.5 kg white fish trimmings and bones, chopped

Makes 2–3 litres

Put all the ingredients except the fish trimmings and bones in a large stockpot. Add water to cover, about 4 litres, and bring to the boil. As soon as it boils, reduce the heat and simmer for 15 minutes. Stir, skim, then add the trimmings and bones. Slowly return to the boil, then reduce the heat and cook at the barest simmer for 20 minutes, skimming often.

Remove from the heat and strain the stock into a bowl through a colander lined with muslin. Discard the contents of the colander when they have cooled. Cool the stock, then refrigerate for several hours, when it should set to a jelly.

At this stage you can reboil the stock to concentrate it, or cover and refrigerate or freeze until needed. The stock will keep in the refrigerator for 2 days or frozen for up to 3 months.

quick seafood stock

brodo leggero di frutti di mare

Although a light fish stock will do, this is a good way to use up any prawn heads or shells, crab or lobster shells you would usually throw away. This stock is quite sweet, unlike a stock made with white fish.

1 onion or ½ leek, chopped

1 celery stalk with leaves, coarsely chopped

a few parsley stalks, lightly crushed

2 bay leaves

2 slices of lemon

4 black peppercorns

75 ml dry white wine

a good pinch of salt

1 kg mixture of seafood pieces (prawn heads or cheap prawns, crab, lobster or crawfish shells)

Makes 2 litres

Put all the ingredients except the seafood pieces in a large stockpot. Add water to cover, about 3 litres, and bring to the boil. As soon as it boils, reduce the heat and simmer for 15 minutes. Stir the stock and skim, then add the seafood pieces. Slowly return to the boil, then reduce the heat and cook at the barest simmer for 20 minutes, skimming often.

Remove from the heat and strain the stock into a bowl through a colander lined with muslin. Discard the contents of the colander when they have cooled. Cool the stock and refrigerate for several hours.

At this stage you can reboil the stock to concentrate it, or cover and chill in the refrigerator or freeze until needed. The stock will keep in the refrigerator for 1–2 days or frozen for up to 3 months.

vegetables

Stirring in real, homemade pesto just before you eat this risotto makes it taste heavenly – quite an explosion on the taste buds. This recipe makes a thick pesto: if you like the idea of a lake of pesto floating over the surface of the risotto, then simply add more olive oil to the mixture. To make good pesto, you must use the right weight of very fresh basil leaves – too little basil and it will taste insipid.

pesto risotto
risotto al pesto

about 1.5 litres hot Light Chicken Stock (page 16) or Vegetable Stock (page 15)

125 g unsalted butter

1 onion, finely chopped

500 g risotto rice

150 ml dry white wine (optional)

sea salt and freshly ground black pepper

pesto genovese

2 garlic cloves

50 g pine nuts

50 g fresh basil leaves

150 ml extra virgin olive oil (or more)

50 g unsalted butter, softened

4 tablespoons freshly grated Parmesan cheese

sea salt and freshly ground black pepper

Serves 6

To make the pesto, use a mortar and pestle to pound the garlic to a cream with a little salt. Add the pine nuts and pound thoroughly. Add the basil leaves a few at a time, pounding and mixing to a paste. Gradually beat in the olive oil until the mixture is creamy and thick. Beat in the butter and season with pepper, then beat in the cheese. Store in a jar in the refrigerator until needed (spoon a layer of olive oil over the top of the pesto to exclude the air.) Alternatively, grind until smooth in a blender or food processor.

Put the stock in a saucepan and keep at a gentle simmer. Melt half the butter in a large, heavy saucepan and add the onion. Cook gently for 10 minutes until soft, golden and translucent but not browned. Add the rice and stir until well coated with butter and heated through. Add the wine, if using, and boil hard until it has been reduced and almost disappeared. This will remove the taste of raw alcohol.

Begin adding the stock, a large ladle at a time, stirring gently until each one has been almost absorbed into the rice. The risotto should be kept at a bare simmer throughout cooking, so don't let the rice dry out – add more stock as necessary. Continue until the rice is tender and creamy, but the grains still firm. (This should take 15–20 minutes, depending on the type of rice used – check the packet instructions.) Taste and season well with salt and pepper and beat in the remaining butter.

Cover and let rest for a couple of minutes so the risotto can relax, then serve immediately. You may like to add a little more hot stock to the risotto just before you serve to loosen it, but don't let it wait too long or the rice will turn mushy. Serve in warm bowls with a large spoonful of pesto in each or spoon liquid pesto over the entire surface before serving.

This simple risotto makes the most of young spinach and peppery rocket, but watercress makes a good alternative if you can't find rocket. Even if you hate anchovies, don't leave them out. They will dissolve into nothing, but add a salty, savoury flavour to the heart of the risotto. If you are a vegetarian, you could add a dash of soy sauce to the stock.

spinach risotto with rocket and roasted tomatoes
risotto con spinaci, rucola e pomodori

about 1.5 litres hot Vegetable Stock (page 15)

125 g unsalted butter

1 onion, finely chopped

1 salted anchovy, boned, split and rinsed, or 2 anchovy fillets in oil

400 g risotto rice

150 ml dry white wine

400 g baby plum tomatoes

4 tablespoons olive oil

200 g young fresh spinach leaves, washed and drained

50 g fresh rocket leaves

sea salt and freshly ground black pepper

freshly grated Parmesan cheese, to serve

Serves 4

Put the stock in a saucepan and keep at a gentle simmer. Melt half the butter in a large, heavy saucepan and add the onion and anchovy. Cook gently for 10 minutes until soft, golden and translucent but not browned. Add the rice and stir until well coated with the butter and heated through. Pour in the wine and boil hard to reduce until it has almost disappeared. This will remove the taste of raw alcohol. Remove from the heat.

Put the tomatoes in a roasting tin and sprinkle with olive oil. Mix well to coat, then season with salt and pepper. Roast in a preheated oven at 200°C (400°F) Gas 6 for about 20 minutes or until slightly collapsed with the skins beginning to brown. Remove from the oven and set aside.

Return the risotto to the heat, warm through and begin adding the stock, a large ladle at a time, stirring gently until each ladle has been almost absorbed into the rice. The risotto should be kept at a bare simmer throughout cooking, so don't let the rice dry out – add more stock as necessary. Continue until the rice is tender and creamy, but the grains still firm. (This should take between 15–20 minutes depending on the type of rice used – check the packet instructions.) Just before the risotto is cooked, stir in the spinach and rocket. Taste and season well with salt and pepper and beat in the remaining butter and the Parmesan. You may like to add a little more hot stock to the risotto at this stage to loosen it.

Cover and let rest for a couple of minutes so the risotto can relax, the cheese melt and the spinach and rocket wilt. Fold in the tomatoes and their juices then serve immediately.

Tomato and rice soup at its best! The risotto is full of the intense flavour of tomatoes, added in three ways: passata to the stock; sun-dried tomatoes adding their caramel flavour deep in the risotto; then tiny ripe plum tomatoes, roasted to perfect sweetness. Delicious hot – but the leftovers are marvellous eaten straight out of the pan.

triple tomato and basil risotto
risotto ai tre pomodori

400 g whole baby plum tomatoes

4 tablespoons olive oil

about 1 litre hot Vegetable Stock (page 15)

500 ml passata (Italian puréed, sieved tomatoes)

125 g unsalted butter

1 onion, finely chopped

8 pieces sun-dried or mi-cuit tomatoes (not the ones in oil), chopped

400 g risotto rice, preferably vialone nano

150 ml light red wine

50 g freshly grated Parmesan cheese

4 tablespoons chopped fresh basil

sea salt and freshly ground black pepper

to serve

extra basil leaves

freshly grated Parmesan cheese

Serves 4

Put the plum tomatoes in a roasting tin and pour over the olive oil. Mix them well to coat and season with salt and pepper. Roast in a preheated oven at 200°C (400°F) Gas 6 for about 20 minutes or until they are slightly collapsed and the skins beginning to brown. Remove from the oven and set aside.

Pour the stock and passata into a saucepan, stir well, then heat to a gentle simmer. Melt half the butter in a large, heavy saucepan and add the onion and chopped sun-dried tomatoes. Cook gently for 10 minutes until soft, golden and translucent but not browned. Add the rice and stir until well coated with the butter and heated through. Pour in the wine and boil hard until it has reduced and almost disappeared. This will remove the taste of raw alcohol. Remove from the heat.

Return the risotto to the heat, warm through, then begin adding the stock, a large ladle at a time, stirring gently until each ladle has almost been absorbed by the rice. The risotto should be kept at a bare simmer throughout cooking, so don't let the rice dry out – add more stock as necessary. Continue until the rice is tender and creamy, but the grains still firm (15–20 minutes depending on the type of rice used – check the packet instructions).

Season to taste with salt and pepper, beat in the remaining butter, the Parmesan and chopped basil. You may like to add a little more hot stock at this stage to loosen the risotto – it should be quite wet. Cover and let rest for a couple of minutes so the risotto can relax and the cheese melt. Carefully ladle into warm bowls and cover the surface with the roasted tomatoes and any juices. Add the basil leaves and serve immediately with extra freshly grated Parmesan cheese.

A spectacular risotto, full of earthy sweetness from finely chopped beetroot. Using raspberry vinegar instead of wine is a good tip, as long as you don't use too much. The raspberry complements the beetroot and the vinegar keeps the red onion nice and pink. I serve this topped with grilled radicchio and melting Fontina cheese for contrast of sweet and bitter.

beetroot risotto
with grilled radicchio
risotto con barbabietole e radicchio arrostito

about 1.5 litres hot Vegetable Stock (page 15)

500 g raw beetroot, peeled and chopped into small cubes

125 g unsalted butter

1 red onion, finely chopped

3 tablespoons raspberry vinegar or red wine vinegar

500 g risotto rice

200 g Fontina cheese, grated

3 tablespoons chopped fresh flat leaf parsley

sea salt and freshly ground black pepper

grilled radicchio (optional)

3 small radicchio, quartered lengthways

100 ml olive oil

Serves 6

Pour the stock into a saucepan and keep at a gentle simmer on top of the stove. Add the beetroot to the stock and simmer for 20–30 minutes until almost tender. Lift out the beetroot with a slotted spoon and set aside.

Melt half the butter in a large, heavy saucepan and add the onion and vinegar. Cook gently for 10 minutes until soft, golden and translucent, but not browned. Add the cooked beetroot, then the rice and stir until well coated with butter and heated through. Begin adding the stock, a large ladle at a time, stirring gently until each ladle has almost been absorbed by the rice. The risotto should be kept at a bare simmer throughout cooking, so don't let the rice dry out – add more stock as necessary. Continue until the rice is tender and creamy, but the grains still firm. (This should take 15–20 minutes depending on the type of rice used – check the packet instructions.) Taste and season well with salt and pepper and beat in the remaining butter, Fontina and parsley. Cover and let rest for a couple of minutes so the risotto can relax and the cheese melt, then serve immediately. You may like to add a little more hot stock to the risotto just before you serve to loosen it, but don't let it wait around too long or the rice will turn mushy.

If serving with the radicchio, heat an overhead grill. Put the radicchio pieces in a grill pan and brush with the oil. Grill for 10–15 minutes until soft and beginning to colour, turning a couple of times. Remove from the grill and set aside. Stir half the Fontina into the risotto before resting. Ladle the risotto into 4 heatproof bowls and top each one with 2 radicchio quarters. Sprinkle with the remaining Fontina, set on a baking tray and grill for 5 minutes until the cheese is melted and bubbling. Serve immediately.

I live in Scotland and was tempted to make a traditional pumpkin risotto using what we call 'turnip' (swede) instead. I was impressed with the result. It was less sweet and cloying than it would be using pumpkin or squash, but had a very distinct flavour. I have served this on Burns' Night on 25th January with haggis, and it is delicious – to my taste anyway – but stick to the traditional recipe and it will be just as good. This tastes wonderful on its own or served with barbecued lamb chops.

butternut squash, sage and chilli risotto

risotto alla zucca, salvia e peperoncino

about 1.5 litres hot Light Chicken Stock (page 16) or Vegetable Stock (page 15)

125 g unsalted butter

1 large onion, finely chopped

1–2 fresh or dried red chillies, deseeded and finely chopped

500 g fresh butternut squash or pumpkin (or swede), peeled and finely diced

500 g risotto rice

3 tablespoons chopped fresh sage

75 g freshly grated Parmesan cheese

sea salt and freshly ground black pepper

Serves 6

Pour the stock into a saucepan and keep at a gentle simmer. Melt half the butter in a large, heavy saucepan and add the onion. Cook gently for 10 minutes until soft, golden and translucent but not browned. Stir in the chopped chillies and cook for 1 minute. Add the butternut or pumpkin, and cook, stirring constantly over the heat for 5 minutes, until it begins to soften slightly. Stir in the rice to coat with the butter and vegetables. Cook for a few minutes to toast the grains.

Begin adding the stock, a large ladle at a time, stirring gently until each ladle has almost been absorbed by the rice. The risotto should be kept at a bare simmer throughout cooking, so don't let the rice dry out – add more stock as necessary. Continue until the rice is tender and creamy, but the grains still firm and the squash beginning to disintegrate. (This should take 15–20 minutes depending on the type of rice used – check the packet instructions.)

Taste and season well with salt and pepper and stir in the sage, remaining butter and all the Parmesan. Cover, let rest for a couple of minutes, then serve immediately.

A pretty orange colur speckled with sweet green peas, this risotto is a delight to eat – the peas pop in your mouth and the seeds give crunch. Fresh peas in season are fantastic, but I am a fan of frozen peas and am never ashamed to use them.

pumpkin and pea risotto
with toasted pumpkin seeds
risotto alla zucca e piselli

125 g unsalted butter

3 tablespoons pumpkin seeds

¼–½ teaspoon ground chilli

about 1 litre hot Vegetable Stock (page 15) or Light Chicken Stock (page 16)

1 large onion, finely chopped

500 g fresh butternut squash or pumpkin, peeled and finely diced

300 g risotto rice

3 tablespoons chopped fresh mint

200 g frozen peas, cooked and drained

75 g freshly grated Parmesan cheese

sea salt and freshly ground black pepper

Serves 6

Put half the butter in a saucepan, melt until foaming, then add the pumpkin seeds. Stir over medium heat until the seeds begin to brown, then stir in the chilli, salt and pepper. Remove from the heat and keep them warm.

Put the stock in a saucepan and keep at a gentle simmer. Melt the remaining butter in a large, heavy saucepan and add the onion. Cook gently for 10 minutes until soft, golden and translucent but not browned. Add the squash or pumpkin, and cook, stirring constantly over the heat for 15 minutes until it begins to soften and disintegrate. Mash the pumpkin in the pan with a potato masher. Stir in the rice to coat with the butter and mashed pumpkin. Cook for a couple of minutes to toast the grains.

Begin adding the stock, a large ladle at a time, stirring gently until each ladle has almost been absorbed by the rice. The risotto should be kept at a bare simmer throughout cooking, so don't let the rice dry out – add more stock as necessary. Continue until the rice is tender and creamy, but the grains still firm. (This should take 15–20 minutes depending on the type of rice used – check the packet instructions.)

Taste and season well with salt and pepper and stir in the mint, peas and all the Parmesan. Cover and let rest for a couple of minutes so the risotto can relax, then serve immediately, sprinkled with the pumpkin seeds. You may like to add a little more hot stock to the risotto just before you serve to loosen it, but don't let it wait around too long or the rice will turn mushy.

A pretty, delicate risotto made even more special with sliced courgette flowers. There are two types of flower – male and female. The female flowers will produce a courgette if fertilized, while the male flowers are the ones used for stuffing. They are just a flower on a stalk and the central spike must be removed before cooking. Courgette flowers are sold in Italian greengrocers and farmers' markets.

courgette flower risotto
risotto con fiori di zucchine

about 1.5 litres hot Light Chicken Stock (page 16) or Vegetable Stock (page 15)

125 g unsalted butter

1 onion, finely chopped

1 celery stalk, finely chopped

400 g risotto rice

4 courgettes, grated

50 g freshly grated Parmesan cheese

4–6 courgette flowers, trimmed and finely sliced

sea salt and freshly ground black pepper

Serves 4

Put the stock in a saucepan and keep at a gentle simmer. Melt half the butter in a large, heavy saucepan and add the onion and celery. Cook gently for 10 minutes until soft, golden and translucent but not browned. Add the rice and stir until well coated with the butter and heated through.

Begin adding the stock, a large ladle at a time, stirring gently until each ladle has almost been absorbed by the rice. The risotto should be kept at a bare simmer throughout cooking, so don't let the rice dry out – add more stock as necessary. Halfway through cooking, stir in the grated courgettes. Continue cooking and adding stock until the rice is tender and creamy, but the grains still firm. (This should take 15–20 minutes, depending on the type of rice used – check the packet instructions.)

Taste and season well with salt and pepper, beat in the remaining butter and all the Parmesan, then stir in the courgette flowers. Cover and let rest for a couple of minutes so the risotto can relax, then serve immediately. You may like to add a little more hot stock to the risotto just before you serve to loosen it, but don't let it wait around too long or the rice will turn mushy.

We make this risotto in our cooking classes in Tuscany in October, when fresh porcini mushrooms are around – and it's a great favourite. Any kind of fresh wild mushroom will make this taste wonderful – black trompettes de mort, deep golden girolles or musky chanterelles. However, it can be made very successfully using a mixture of cultivated mushrooms and dried reconstituted Italian porcini or French cèpes. In Italy, a wild herb called *nepitella* is often used when cooking wild mushrooms. It is a type of wild catnip and complements the mushrooms very well.

wild mushroom risotto
risotto ai funghi di bosco

1.5 litres hot Light Chicken Stock (page 16) or Vegetable Stock (page 15)

125 g unsalted butter

1 large onion, finely chopped

2 garlic cloves, finely chopped

250 g mixed wild mushrooms, cleaned and coarsely chopped (or a mixture of wild and fresh, or 200 g cultivated mushrooms, plus 25 g dried porcini soaked in warm water for 20 minutes, drained and chopped)

1 tablespoon each of chopped fresh thyme and marjoram (or *nepitella*)

150 ml dry white wine or vermouth

500 g risotto rice

75 g freshly grated Parmesan cheese, plus extra to serve

sea salt and freshly ground black pepper

Serves 6

Put the stock in a saucepan and keep at a gentle simmer. Melt the butter in a large, heavy saucepan and add the onion and garlic. Cook gently for 10 minutes until soft, golden and translucent but not browned. Stir in the mushrooms and herbs, then cook over medium heat for 3 minutes to heat through. Pour in the wine and boil hard until it has reduced and almost disappeared. This will remove the taste of raw alcohol. Stir in the rice and fry with the onion and mushrooms until dry and slightly opaque.

Begin adding the stock, a large ladle at a time, stirring until each ladle has been absorbed by the rice. Continue until the rice is tender and creamy, but the grains still firm. (This should take 15–20 minutes depending on the type of rice used – check the packet instructions.)

Taste and season well with salt and pepper. Stir in the Parmesan, cover and let rest for a couple of minutes. Serve immediately with extra grated Parmesan.

When the Italian asparagus season is in full flush, it is celebrated with great gusto. Asparagus of all types is for sale, the most prized being the fat white asparagus. It is usually cooked further than *al dente*, which really brings out the flavour. This is about the only time I like to have shaved Parmesan on a risotto – the contrast of textures is wonderful.

asparagus risotto
with a poached egg and parmesan
risotto agli asparagi con uovo in camicia e parmigiano

500 g fresh green or purple-tipped asparagus

about 1.5 litres hot Vegetable Stock (page 15) or Light Chicken Stock (page 16)

1 teaspoon tarragon wine vinegar or white wine vinegar

6 fresh eggs, cracked into separate cups

125 g unsalted butter

2 large shallots, finely chopped

500 g risotto rice, preferably carnaroli

50 g freshly grated Parmesan cheese

sea salt and freshly ground black pepper

to serve

1 tablespoon chopped fresh parsley and tarragon, mixed

Parmesan shavings

Serves 6

Trim the base from each asparagus stem, but do no more than that. Put the stock in a wide saucepan and heat to simmering. Add the asparagus and boil for about 6 minutes until just tender. Drain, reserving the asparagus-flavoured stock and transferring it to a regular saucepan to simmer. Plunge the asparagus into a bowl of cold water to cool and set the colour, then cut into small pieces. If the ends of the asparagus stalks are very tough, cut them off, halve them and scrape out the insides and reserve. Add the tough parts to the stock. Reserve a few tips to serve.

To poach the eggs, fill a medium saucepan with cold water and bring to the boil. When the water is boiling, add the wine vinegar, then give it a good stir to create a whirlpool. Slip an egg into the vortex, then simmer very gently for 2–3 minutes. Using a slotted spoon, transfer the poached egg to a pan of warm water. Repeat the same procedure with the other eggs. Keep them warm while you make the risotto.

Melt half the butter in a large, heavy saucepan and add the shallots. Cook gently for 5–6 minutes until soft, golden and translucent but not browned. Add the rice and asparagus scrapings to the shallots and stir until well coated with the butter and heated through. Begin adding the stock, a large ladle at a time (keeping back the asparagus trimmings), stirring gently until each ladle has almost been absorbed by the rice. The risotto should be kept at a bare simmer throughout cooking, so don't let the rice dry out – add more stock as necessary. Continue until the rice is tender and creamy, but the grains still firm. (This should take 15–20 minutes depending on the type of rice used – check the packet instructions.)

Taste and season well with salt and pepper and beat in the remaining butter and all the Parmesan. Fold in the drained asparagus. Cover, let rest for a few minutes so the risotto can relax and the asparagus heat through, then serve immediately. You may like to add a little more hot stock to the risotto just before you serve to loosen it, but don't let it wait around too long or the rice will turn mushy. Serve the risotto topped with a drained poached egg, sprinkled with parsley and tarragon and Parmesan shavings.

The secret of this risotto is not to cut the vegetables too big – they should be jewel-like in the risotto. Sometimes, I stir half into the risotto and pile the rest on top. Sprinkle the risotto with basil leaves and trickle good olive oil over the top before serving.

oven-roasted mediterranean vegetable risotto

risotto con verdure del mediterraneo

1 courgette, trimmed and cut into 2 cm chunks

1 aubergine, trimmed and cut into 2 cm chunks

1 red pepper, halved, deseeded and cut into squares

1 carrot, cut into sticks

100 ml olive oil

about 1.5 litres hot Vegetable Stock (page 15)

100 g unsalted butter

1 red onion, finely chopped

2 garlic cloves, finely chopped

1 tablespoon freshly squeezed lemon juice

1 teaspoon crushed coriander seeds

a pinch of chilli powder

500 g risotto rice

150 ml dry white wine

3 tablespoons finely sliced fresh basil

sea salt and freshly ground black pepper

to serve

basil leaves

freshly grated Parmesan cheese

extra virgin olive oil

Serves 6

Put the courgette, aubergine, pepper and carrot into a large roasting tin, add the oil and 100 ml water and toss well to coat. Roast in a preheated oven at 200°C (400°F) Gas 6 for about 25 minutes, turning often until the vegetables are tender and caramelizing. Remove from the oven and tip into a colander set over a bowl. Reserve the cooking juices. Cool the vegetables.

Put the stock in a saucepan and keep at a gentle simmer. Melt half the butter in a large, heavy saucepan and add the onion, garlic and the lemon juice. Cook gently for 10 minutes until soft, golden and translucent but not browned. Add the coriander seeds and chilli, then the rice and stir until well coated with the butter and heated through. Pour in the reserved roasting juices and wine and boil hard until they have reduced and almost disappeared. This will remove the taste of raw alcohol.

Begin adding the stock, a large ladle at a time, stirring gently until each ladle has almost been absorbed by the rice. The risotto should be kept at a bare simmer throughout cooking, so don't let the rice dry out – add more stock as necessary. Continue until the rice is tender and creamy, but the grains still firm. (This should take 15–20 minutes depending on the type of rice used – check the packet instructions.)

Taste and season well with salt and pepper and beat in the rest of the butter. Reserve a few spoonfuls of the vegetables, then fold in the remainder and the basil, cover and let rest for a few minutes so the risotto can relax and the vegetables heat through. Serve immediately. You may like to add a little more hot stock to the risotto just before you serve to loosen it, but don't let it wait around too long or the rice will turn mushy.

Top with the basil, reserved vegetables, Parmesan and a trickle of olive oil.

Smoky char-grilled artichokes are wonderful combined with nutty pecorino. Pecorino is made from ewes' milk (*latte de pecora*) and when aged can be grated like Parmesan. When young, it has a Cheddar-like texture and a rich, nutty flavour.

artichoke and pecorino risotto
risotto ai carciofi e pecorino

12 fresh artichokes, or 12 char-grilled deli artichokes, or 8 frozen artichoke bottoms, thawed

about 1.5 litres hot Light Chicken Stock (page 16) or Vegetable Stock (page 15)

125 g unsalted butter, plus extra for frying (optional)
1 onion, finely chopped

500 g risotto rice

150 ml dry white wine

75 g freshly grated pecorino cheese

sea salt and freshly ground black pepper

Serves 4

First prepare the fresh artichokes, if using (see below), then brush with olive oil and char-grill for 5 minutes on a stove-top grill pan, turning often. If using char-grilled ones from the deli, cut them in quarters and set aside. If using thawed frozen ones, slice them and fry in a little butter until golden.

Put the stock in a saucepan and keep at a gentle simmer. Melt 65 g of the butter in a large, heavy saucepan and add the onion. Cook gently for 10 minutes until soft, golden and translucent but not browned. Add the rice and stir until well coated with the butter and heated through. Pour in the wine and boil hard until it has reduced and almost disappeared. This will remove the taste of raw alcohol.

Begin adding the stock, a large ladle at a time, stirring gently until each ladle has almost been absorbed by the rice. The risotto should be kept at a bare simmer throughout cooking, so don't let the rice dry out – add more stock as necessary. Continue until the rice is tender and creamy, but the grains still firm. (This should take 15–20 minutes depending on the type of rice used – check the packet instructions.)

Taste and season well with salt and pepper and beat in the remaining butter and all the pecorino. Fold in the artichokes. Cover and let rest for a couple of minutes so the risotto can relax, then serve immediately. You may like to add a little more hot stock to the risotto just before you serve to loosen it, but don't let it wait around too long or the rice will turn mushy.

Note To prepare fresh young artichokes, you will need 1 lemon, halved, and purple-green baby artichokes with stems and heads, about 10 cm long. Fill a large bowl with water and squeeze in the juice of ½ lemon to acidulate it. Use the other lemon half to rub the cut portions of the artichoke as you work. Trim the artichokes by snapping off the dark outer leaves, starting at the base. Trim the stalk down to about 5 cm. Trim away the green outer layer at the base and peel the fibrous outside of the stalk with a vegetable peeler. Cut about 1 cm off the tip of each artichoke heart. Put each artichoke in the lemony water until needed – this will stop them discolouring. Drain and use as required.

A wonderfully light and fragrant risotto, perfect for the summer to serve with cold chicken or fish. Try to use the more fragrant soft herbs here – the more the merrier.

green herb risotto
with white wine and lemon
risotto alle erbe verdi e limone

about 1.5 litres hot Vegetable Stock (page 15) or Light Chicken Stock (page 16)

125 g unsalted butter

8 spring onions, green and white parts, finely chopped

150 ml dry white wine

finely grated zest and juice of 1 large unwaxed lemon

500 g risotto rice

4 tablespoons chopped fresh herbs such as parsley, basil, marjoram and thyme

75 g freshly grated Parmesan cheese

sea salt and freshly ground black pepper

Serves 4–6

Put the stock in a saucepan and keep at a gentle simmer. Melt half the butter in a large, heavy saucepan and add the spring onions. Cook gently for 3–5 minutes until soft. Pour in the wine, add half the lemon zest and boil hard until the wine has reduced and almost disappeared. This will remove the taste of raw alcohol. Add the rice and stir until well coated with butter and onions and heated through.

Begin to add the hot stock, a large ladle at a time, stirring until each ladle has been absorbed by the rice. Continue until the rice is tender and creamy, but the grains still firm. (This should take 15–20 minutes depending on the type of rice used – check the packet instructions.)

Taste and season well with salt and lots of freshly ground black pepper. Stir in the remaining butter, the lemon zest, juice, herbs and Parmesan. Cover and let rest for a couple of minutes, then serve immediately.

Carrots are an underestimated vegetable. When in their prime, they are sweet and juicy and roast perfectly. The watercress pesto, which looks spectacular with the orange risotto, has a nutty, peppery taste. Rocket could be used instead of watercress with the same peppery result.

caramelized carrot risotto
with watercress pesto
risotto con carote arrostite e pesto al crescione

500 g carrots, peeled, then cut into chunky rounds or batons

4 tablespoons olive oil

sea salt and freshly ground black pepper

watercress pesto

50 g watercress leaves, without stalks

1 garlic clove, chopped

3 tablespoons freshly grated Parmesan cheese

25 g shelled hazelnuts

90 ml extra virgin olive oil, plus extra for covering

sea salt and freshly ground black pepper

risotto

about 1.5 litres hot Vegetable Stock (page 15) or Light Chicken Stock (page 16)

125 g unsalted butter

1 onion, finely chopped

400 g risotto rice

150 ml dry white wine

75 g freshly grated Parmesan cheese

sea salt and freshly ground black pepper

Serves 4

Toss the carrots in the olive oil, spread in a roasting tin and sprinkle with salt and pepper. Roast in a preheated oven at 200°C (400°F) Gas 6 for 20 minutes, turning occasionally until they begin to caramelize.

Meanwhile, to make the pesto, put the watercress, garlic, Parmesan, hazelnuts, olive oil, salt and pepper in a food processor and blend until smooth, scraping down any bits that cling to the side of the bowl. Alternatively, pound with a mortar and pestle. Cover with a thin layer of oil and set aside.

To make the risotto, put the stock in a saucepan and keep at a gentle simmer. Melt half the butter in a large, heavy saucepan and add the onion. Cook gently for 10 minutes until soft, golden and translucent but not browned. Add the rice and stir until well coated with the butter and heated through. Pour in the wine and boil hard until it has reduced and almost disappeared. This will remove the taste of raw alcohol.

Begin adding the stock, a large ladle at a time, stirring gently until each ladle has almost been absorbed by the rice. The risotto should be kept at a bare simmer throughout cooking, so don't let the rice dry out – add more stock as necessary. Continue until the rice is tender and creamy, but the grains still firm. (This should take 15–20 minutes depending on the type of rice used – check the packet instructions.) Stir in the carrots and pan juices. Add salt and pepper to taste and beat in the remaining butter and half the Parmesan.

Cover and let rest for a few minutes so the risotto can relax and the cheese melt, then serve immediately. You may like to add a little more hot stock to the risotto just before you serve to loosen it, but don't let it wait around too long or the rice will turn mushy. Serve in warm bowls with a spoon of pesto on top and sprinkled with the remaining Parmesan.

A delicate fennel and lemon risotto with the taste of the Mediterranean stirred in just before serving. I like the rich earthiness of shiny, oven-dried black olives, but if you prefer something less pungent, use large, juicy green olives instead.

fennel and black olive risotto

risotto ai finocchi con olive nere

fennel and black olive relish

6 tablespoons extra virgin olive oil

1 onion, finely chopped

1 garlic clove, crushed

1 fennel bulb, trimmed and chopped

5 sun-dried tomatoes in oil, drained and coarsely chopped

200 g oven-dried (Greek-style) olives, pitted

1 fresh bay leaf

12 basil leaves, torn

2 tablespoons aniseed liqueur, such as Sambuca

sea salt and freshly ground black pepper

fennel risotto

about 1 litre hot Vegetable Stock (page 15) or Light Chicken Stock (page 16)

125 g unsalted butter

1 onion, finely chopped

3 fennel bulbs, trimmed and finely chopped (green tops included)

finely grated zest of 1 unwaxed lemon

300 g risotto rice

150 ml dry white wine

freshly grated Parmesan cheese, to serve

Serves 6

To make the relish, heat 2 tablespoons of the olive oil in a medium saucepan and gently cook the onion, garlic and fennel for a few minutes until softening. Add the sun-dried tomatoes, olives and bay leaf and continue to cook for 2–3 minutes more. Season to taste with salt and pepper, remove the bay leaf, then stir in the basil. Transfer to a food processor and blend to a coarse texture. Stir in the aniseed liqueur and remaining olive oil. Cover and set aside.

To make the risotto, put the stock in a saucepan and keep at a gentle simmer. Melt half the butter in a large, heavy saucepan and add the onion. Cook gently for 5 minutes until soft, golden and translucent, but not browned. Stir in the fennel and lemon zest and continue to cook for 10 minutes until softening. Add the rice and stir until well coated with the butter and heated through. Pour in the wine and boil hard until it has reduced and almost disappeared. This will remove the taste of raw alcohol.

Begin adding the stock, a large ladle at a time, stirring gently until each ladle has almost been absorbed by the rice. The risotto should be kept at a bare simmer throughout cooking, so don't let the rice dry out – add more stock as necessary. Continue until the rice is tender and creamy, but the grains still firm and the fennel absolutely tender. (This should take 15–20 minutes depending on the type of rice used – check the packet instructions.)

Taste and season well with salt and pepper and beat in the remaining butter. Cover and let rest for a couple of minutes so the risotto can relax, then serve immediately. Just before serving, you may like to add a little more hot stock to loosen the risotto, but don't let it wait around too long or the rice will turn mushy. Top with the fennel and black olive relish before serving with extra grated Parmesan.

A lovely soup to serve in the summer when fresh peas are in abundance. Vialone nano is the favourite rice for risotto in the Veneto region. It is a *semifino* round grain rice, best for soup and risotto, but arborio, a *superfino* used mainly for risotto, will do very nicely. This has very ancient roots, and was flavoured with fennel seeds at one time. Parsley is the usual addition, but I prefer mint in the summer.

venetian pea and rice thick soup
risi e bisi

1 kg fresh peas in the pod or 400 g frozen peas

1.2 litres hot Light Chicken Stock (page 16), Beef Stock (page 19) or Vegetable Stock (page 15)

2 tablespoons olive oil

60 g unsalted butter

50 g pancetta, finely chopped

1 large cipollotto* or the white parts of 4 spring onions, finely chopped

200 g risotto rice, preferably vialone nano

3 tablespoons chopped fresh parsley or mint

freshly grated Parmesan cheese

sea salt and freshly ground black pepper

Serves 4

Cipollotto is a delicious Italian onion, a little like a large spring onion. Use a regular onion, a salad onion or spring onions if unavailable.

Shell the peas and set aside. Slowly bring the stock to the boil with the pea pods (if using) while you prepare the pancetta and onion base.

Heat the olive oil with half the butter and, when melted, add the pancetta and onion. Cook for about 5 minutes but do not let it brown. Add the rice, stir for a few minutes to toast it, then add the hot stock. Simmer for 10 minutes, stirring from time to time, then add the peas, cook for another 5–7 minutes, then stir in the remaining butter, parsley or mint and Parmesan.

Taste and season with salt and pepper and serve immediately. The rice grains should not be too mushy, and the soup should be thick and soupy, but not at all stodgy. Add more stock or water if necessary to thin it down.

The charm of this risotto is found in the delicate flavours and colours of spring. The vegetables are small and sweet, the herbs fresh and fragrant. Don't be tempted to skimp on the herbs here – as well as imparting intense flavour to the risotto, they add a beautiful touch of spring green. Sometimes I blend them with the remaining butter (melted) to give a bright green liquid to beat in at the end.

spring risotto with herbs
risotto primavera alle erbe

about 1.5 litres hot Light Chicken Stock (page 16) or Vegetable Stock (page 15)

125 g unsalted butter

6 spring onions, finely chopped

2 garlic cloves, finely chopped, crushed

150 g carrots, cubed, or a bunch of tiny new carrots, trimmed and scraped but kept whole

400 g risotto rice, preferably carnaroli

100 g asparagus spears, trimmed and cut into 2 cm lengths

100 g fine green beans, cut into 2 cm lengths

100 g fresh or frozen peas or broad beans, thawed if frozen

6 tablespoons chopped mixed fresh herbs, such as chives, dill, flat leaf parsley, mint, chervil and tarragon

50 g freshly grated Parmesan cheese, plus extra to serve

sea salt and freshly ground black pepper

Serves 4

Put the stock in a saucepan and keep at a gentle simmer. Melt half the butter in a large, heavy saucepan and add the spring onions, garlic and carrots. Cook gently for 5 minutes until the onions are soft and translucent but not browned. Stir in the rice until well coated with the butter and heated through.

Begin adding the stock, a large ladle at a time, stirring gently until each ladle has almost been absorbed by the rice. The risotto should be kept at a bare simmer throughout cooking, so don't let the rice dry out – add more stock as necessary. After 10 minutes, add the asparagus, beans and peas and continue until the vegetables are tender and the rice is tender and creamy, but the grains still firm. (This should take 15–20 minutes depending on the type of rice used – check the packet instructions.)

Taste and season well with salt and pepper and stir in the remaining butter and the herbs. Cover and let rest for a couple of minutes so the risotto can relax, then serve immediately with extra freshly grated Parmesan cheese. You may like to add a little more hot stock to the risotto just before you serve to loosen it, but don't let it wait around too long or the rice will turn mushy.

A dish from the Veneto, where vialone nano rice is grown, as well as several varieties of radicchio. Stirring in a good spoonful of mascarpone or cream at the end enriches the risotto and adds sweetness. The risotto has both a sweet and a bitter flavour. I like to add a few currants plumped up for 20 minutes in warm grappa for an added surprise.

creamy radicchio and mascarpone risotto

risotto cremoso al radicchio e mascarpone

about 1.5 litres hot Light Chicken Stock (page 16) or Vegetable Stock (page 15)

125 g unsalted butter

2 carrots, finely diced

125 g smoked pancetta, finely diced

2 garlic cloves, finely chopped

500 g radicchio, finely shredded

500 g risotto rice

2 tablespoons currants soaked in 4 tablespoons warm grappa for 20 minutes (optional)

3 tablespoons mascarpone cheese or double cream

75 g freshly grated Parmesan cheese

sea salt and freshly ground black pepper

Serves 6

Put the stock in a saucepan and keep at a gentle simmer. Melt half the butter in a large, heavy saucepan and add the carrots. Cook gently for 5 minutes until softening. Add the pancetta and garlic, and cook for 4 minutes until just beginning to colour. Stir in the radicchio and cook for 5 minutes until it begins to wilt. Add the rice and stir until heated through. Add a ladle of hot stock and simmer, stirring until absorbed. Continue adding the stock ladle by ladle, making sure the rice is never dry, until all the stock is absorbed. The rice should be tender and creamy but still have some bite to it. (This should take 15–20 minutes depending on the type of rice used – check the packet instructions.)

Taste and season well with salt and plenty of freshly ground black pepper. Add the soaked currants, if using, and stir in the remaining butter, the mascarpone or cream and the Parmesan. Cover and let rest for a couple of minutes, then serve immediately.

An amazing risotto to serve on its own as a first course or to accompany meat or game dishes. This risotto needs the sweetness of the vegetables to balance the acidity from the wine. Use a good wine that you would not be ashamed to drink, and you will achieve perfect results. Use a cheap, undrinkable wine and the risotto will be inedible. Brighten it up with a scattering of emerald green chopped parsley.

red wine risotto
risotto al barolo

about 1.5 litres Vegetable (page 15) or Light Chicken Stock (page 16)

125 g unsalted butter

1 small red onion, finely chopped

1 small carrot, finely chopped

1 small celery stalk, finely chopped

50 g pancetta, finely chopped (optional)

500 g risotto rice

300 ml full-bodied red wine such as Barolo

125 g freshly grated Parmesan cheese

sea salt and freshly ground black pepper

chopped fresh parsley, to serve

Serves 4–6

Put the stock in a saucepan and keep at a gentle simmer. Melt half the butter in a large, heavy saucepan and add the onion, carrot and celery. Cook gently for 10 minutes until soft, golden and translucent but not browned. Add the pancetta (if using) and cook for another 2 minutes. Add the rice and stir until well coated with the butter and heated through. Pour in the wine and boil hard until it has been reduced by half. This will remove the taste of raw alcohol.

Begin adding the stock, a large ladle at a time, stirring gently until each ladle has almost been absorbed by the rice. The risotto should be kept at a bare simmer throughout cooking, so don't let the rice dry out – add more stock as necessary. Continue until the rice is tender and creamy, but the grains still firm. (This should take 15–20 minutes depending on the type of rice used – check the packet instructions.)

Taste and season well with salt and pepper and beat in the remaining butter and all the Parmesan. Cover and let rest for a couple of minutes so the risotto can relax, then serve immediately. You may like to add a little more hot stock to the risotto just before you serve to loosen it, but don't let it wait around too long or the rice will turn mushy. Serve sprinkled with parsley.

cheese and eggs

When you have nothing except risotto rice in the cupboard, and a chunk of Parmesan and some butter in the refrigerator, yet feel the need for comfort and luxury, this is the risotto for you. It is pale, golden, smooth and creamy and relies totally on the quality of the rice, butter and cheese. I would use real Parmigiano Reggiano, with its sweet, nutty flavour, and nothing else.

parmesan and butter risotto
risotto alla parmigiana

about 1.5 litres hot Light Chicken Stock (page 16) or Vegetable Stock (page 15)

150 g unsalted butter

1 onion, finely chopped

500 g risotto rice, preferably carnaroli

150 ml dry white wine

100 g freshly grated Parmesan cheese

sea salt and freshly ground black pepper

Serves 4–6

Put the stock in a saucepan and keep at a gentle simmer. Melt half the butter in a large, heavy saucepan and add the onion. Cook gently for 10 minutes until soft, golden and translucent but not browned. Add the rice and stir until well coated with the butter and heated through. Pour in the wine and boil hard until it has reduced and almost disappeared. This will remove any raw alcohol taste.

Begin adding the stock, a large ladle at a time, stirring gently until each ladle has almost been absorbed by the rice. The risotto should be kept at a bare simmer throughout cooking, so don't let the rice dry out – add more stock as necessary. Continue until the rice is tender and creamy, but the grains still firm. (This should take 15–20 minutes depending on the type of rice used – check the packet instructions.)

Taste and season well with salt and pepper, then stir in the remaining butter and all the Parmesan. Cover and let rest for a couple of minutes so the risotto can relax and the cheese melt, then serve immediately. You may like to add a little more stock just before you serve, but don't let the risotto wait around too long or the rice will turn mushy.

This is not to be confused with *risotto alla milanese,* which accompanies the famous dish *osso buco,* enriched with delicious beef bone marrow. However, this recipe does the job very nicely, producing a rich, creamy risotto with the delicate taste of saffron. Saffron powder can also be used, but make sure it is real saffron and not just ground stamens of the safflower. Saffron will always be relatively expensive when bought outside its country of origin, and is a great thing to take home with you if you are visiting Italy or Spain, where it can be found at a good price.

saffron risotto

risotto allo zafferano

about 1.5 litres hot Light Chicken Stock (page 16) or Vegetable Stock (page 15)

125 g unsalted butter

1 onion, finely chopped

500 g risotto rice

150 ml dry white wine

16 saffron threads or ½ teaspoon ground saffron

75 g freshly grated Parmesan cheese

sea salt and freshly ground black pepper

Serves 4–6

Put the stock in a saucepan and keep at a gentle simmer. Melt half the butter in a large, heavy saucepan and add the onion. Cook gently for 10 minutes until soft, golden and translucent but not browned. Add the rice and stir until well coated with the butter and heated through. Pour in the wine and boil hard until it has reduced and almost disappeared. This will remove any raw alcohol taste.

Begin adding the stock, a large ladle at a time, adding the saffron after the first ladle. Stir gently until each ladle has almost been absorbed by the rice. The risotto should be kept at a bare simmer throughout cooking, so don't let the rice dry out – add more stock as necessary. Continue until the rice is tender and creamy, but the grains still firm. (This should take 15–20 minutes depending on the type of rice used – check the packet instructions.)

Taste and season well with salt and pepper and stir in the remaining butter and all the Parmesan. Cover and let rest for a couple of minutes so the risotto can relax, then serve immediately. You may like to add a little more stock just before serving to loosen it, but don't let the risotto wait around too long or the rice will turn mushy.

When you dip your fork into this risotto, you will come across pockets of melting mozzarella. Mix in the tomato topping and you will make more strings. Try to use *mozzarella di bufala* – it has a fresh, lactic bite well-suited to this recipe.

mozzarella and sun-blushed tomato risotto with basil
risotto con mozzarella e pomodori semi-secchi

about 1.5 litres hot Light Chicken Stock
(page 16) or Vegetable Stock (page 15)

125 g unsalted butter

1 onion, finely chopped

400 g risotto rice

150 ml dry white wine

250 g mozzarella cheese, cut into 1 cm cubes

4 tablespoons chopped fresh basil

300 g sun-blushed tomatoes

sea salt and freshly ground black pepper

to serve

extra basil leaves

freshly grated Parmesan cheese

Serves 4

Put the stock in a saucepan and keep at a gentle simmer. Melt half the butter in a large, heavy saucepan and add the onion. Cook gently for 10 minutes until soft, golden and translucent but not browned. Add the rice and stir until well coated with the butter and heated through. Pour in the wine and boil hard until it has reduced and almost disappeared. This will remove the taste of raw alcohol.

Begin adding the stock, a large ladle at a time, stirring gently until each ladle has almost been absorbed by the rice. The risotto should be kept at a bare simmer throughout cooking, so don't let the rice dry out – add more stock as necessary. Continue until the rice is tender and creamy, but the grains still firm. (This should take 15–20 minutes depending on the type of rice used – check the packet instructions.)

Taste and season well with salt and pepper and beat in the remaining butter. You may like to add a little more hot stock at this stage to loosen the risotto. Fold in the cubed mozzarella and chopped basil. Cover and let rest for a couple of minutes so the risotto can relax and the cheese melt. Carefully ladle into warm bowls and put a pile of tomatoes in the centre of each one. Top with basil leaves and serve immediately with a bowl of grated Parmesan.

Gorgonzola is a strong cheese with blue-green marbling. The mould is injected into the cheese and left in temperature-controlled store rooms or caves. Factory-made cheese tends to be firmer, with a regular crazing of blue-green. Artisan or farm-made Gorgonzola, left in caves to develop the injected mould naturally, produces a creamy, less densely marbled cheese. In Italy, you buy Gorgonzola either *dolce* or *piccante* – mild or strong. I like *piccante*. Dolcelatte is made for the export market.

gorgonzola and ricotta risotto
with crisp sage leaves
risotto al gorgonzola, ricotta e salvia

about 1.5 litres hot Light Chicken Stock (page 16) or Vegetable Stock (page 15)

125 g unsalted butter

1 onion, finely chopped

400 g risotto rice

75 ml dry white vermouth

1 tablespoon chopped fresh sage leaves

75 g Gorgonzola cheese, crumbled

75 g fresh ricotta cheese

sea salt and freshly ground black pepper

crisp sage leaves

about 30 sage leaves with stalks

sea salt

oil, for deep frying

electric deep-fryer or wok

Serves 4

To make the crisp sage leaves, pat them thoroughly dry. Heat the oil to 180°C (350°F) in a deep-fryer or wok. If using a fryer, put the leaves in the basket and lower into the oil. It will hiss alarmingly, but don't worry. Immediately the hissing has stopped, lift the basket out and shake off the excess oil. (If using a wok, use tongs or a slotted spoon.) Put the leaves on kitchen paper to drain. Season with a sprinkling of salt and set aside. They will crisp up as they cool.

Put the stock in a saucepan and keep at a gentle simmer. Melt half the butter in a large, heavy saucepan and add the onion. Cook gently for 10 minutes until soft, golden and translucent but not browned. Add the rice and stir until well coated with the butter and heated through. Pour in the vermouth and boil hard until reduced and almost disappeared. This will remove the taste of raw alcohol. Stir in the chopped fresh sage.

Begin adding the stock, a large ladle at a time, stirring gently until each ladle has almost been absorbed by the rice. The risotto should be kept at a bare simmer throughout cooking, so don't let the rice dry out – add more stock as necessary. About halfway through the cooking time, stir in the Gorgonzola until melted. Continue adding stock and cooking until the rice is tender and creamy, but the grains still firm. (This should take 15–20 minutes depending on the type of rice used – check the packet instructions.) The risotto should be quite loose, but not soupy.

Taste and season well with salt and pepper and beat in the ricotta and remaining butter. Cover and let rest for a couple of minutes so the risotto can relax. You may like to add a little more hot stock to the risotto just before you serve to loosen it, but don't let it wait around too long or the rice will turn mushy. Serve with the fried sage leaves on top.

A risotto made with meltingly soft Fontina cheese or even raclette becomes almost a fondue. Bresaola is often served as a side dish with raclette and fondue, and makes a delicious topping to the risotto. Produced around Valtellina in Lombardy, bresaola is raw fillet of beef, salted then air-dried. It is always sliced very thinly and is a beautiful, deep garnet-red colour. Freshly cut bresaola is best, it is soft and sweet, whereas the layered kind in packets tends to be a bit dry.

raclette or fontina risotto
with bresaola
risotto alla raclette o fontina con bresaola

about 1.5 litres hot Vegetable Stock (page 15) or Light Chicken Stock (page 16)

125 g unsalted butter

1 onion, finely chopped

500 g risotto rice

150 ml fruity white wine

100 g Fontina or raclette cheese, rinds removed and remainder grated or chopped

6–8 thin slices bresaola, finely chopped, plus 8–12 thin slices extra, to serve

sea salt and freshly ground black pepper

Serves 4–6

Put the stock in a saucepan and keep at a gentle simmer. Melt half the butter in a large, heavy saucepan and add the onion. Cook gently for 10 minutes until soft, golden and translucent but not browned. Add the rice and stir until well coated with the butter and heated through. Pour in the wine and boil hard until it has reduced and almost disappeared. This will remove the taste of raw alcohol.

Begin adding the stock, a large ladle at a time, stirring gently until each ladle has almost been absorbed by the rice. The risotto should be kept at a bare simmer throughout cooking, so don't let the rice dry out – add more stock as necessary. Halfway through cooking, stir in the cheese until melted. Continue adding stock and cooking until the rice is tender and creamy, but the grains still firm. (This should take 15–20 minutes depending on the type of rice used – check the packet instructions.)

Taste and season well with salt and pepper and beat in the remaining butter and chopped bresaola. Cover and let rest for a couple of minutes so the risotto can relax. You may like to add a little more hot stock to the risotto just before you serve to loosen it, but don't let it wait around too long or the rice will turn mushy. The risotto should be quite loose. Serve with the remaining bresaola crumpled or draped on top.

Roasting a big batch of garlic makes sure that you will always have some in the refrigerator for adding to soups or even spreading on toast or bruschetta. I use two kinds of cheese here. The soft cheese melts creamily into the risotto, whereas the cheese with rind (*Bûcheron chèvre*) cut from a thick log, grills to perfection without collapsing – as long as it isn't too ripe.

roasted garlic risotto
with goats' cheese and rosemary
risotto con caprino, aglio dorato e rosmarino

20 large garlic cloves, peeled (you will only use 8, but you can keep the rest in a jar of oil in the refrigerator)

75 ml extra virgin olive oil, plus extra for basting

4–6 large thick slices goats' cheese with rind

4–6 small sprigs of rosemary, plus extra to serve

about 1.5 litres hot Light Chicken Stock (page 16)

1 red onion, finely chopped

2 tablespoons chopped fresh rosemary

500 g risotto rice

200 g soft mild goats' cheese (the one with no rind)

50 g freshly grated Parmesan cheese

sea salt and freshly ground black pepper

30 cm square of kitchen foil

a baking sheet

non-stick baking parchment

Serves 4–6

Put the garlic, 2 tablespoons of oil, salt and pepper in a mixing bowl and toss well. Put the garlic in the middle of the foil, fold up the long ends and fold together at the top to create a seal. Fold in the short ends to create a sealed packet. Set on a baking sheet and roast in a preheated oven at 180°C (350°F) Gas 4 for 20 minutes, then turn over, cut a small steam hole in the top (former underside) and roast the packet upside down for a further 10 minutes. (This will keep wrapped tightly in the refrigerator for up to 1 week.) Reserve 8 cloves to use.

Put the sliced goats' cheese on a grill pan lined with the parchment. Brush with olive oil and put a rosemary sprig on each one. Sprinkle with pepper and set aside. Preheat the grill.

Put the stock in a saucepan and keep at a gentle simmer. Heat the remaining olive oil in a heavy saucepan. Add the onion and cook gently for 5 minutes. Add the roasted garlic and half the chopped rosemary. Cook for a further 5 minutes, then stir in the rice until well coated with oil and heated through.

Begin adding the stock, a large ladle at a time, stirring gently until each ladle has almost been absorbed by the rice. The risotto should be kept at a bare simmer throughout cooking, so don't let the rice dry out – add more stock as necessary. Halfway through cooking the risotto, grill the sliced goats' cheese until browned on top. Continue until the rice is tender and creamy, but the grains still firm. (This should take 15–20 minutes depending on the type of rice used – check the packet instructions.) Stir in the soft cheese and remaining rosemary.

Taste and season well with salt and pepper and beat in the Parmesan cheese. Cover and let rest for a couple of minutes so the risotto can relax, then serve immediately in warm bowls. You may like to add a little more hot stock to the risotto just before you serve to loosen it, but don't let it wait around too long or the rice will turn mushy. Using a palette knife or spatula, set a slice of grilled goats' cheese on each serving and top with a sprig of rosemary.

This is a way of enjoying the taste of truffles without the enormous expense. Fresh white truffles from Alba are heaven shaved over a white risotto, but there are lots of products flavoured with truffles. There's truffle butter, truffle oil (make sure it is the real thing and not just flavoured with a chemical) and truffle paste or sauce. All these can be mixed with egg yolks, then added to the risotto as long as you don't add too much – it can be very overpowering. Parsley brings the whole thing alive and the best parsley in Italy is said to come from Lombardy.

truffled egg risotto
risotto all'uovo e tartufi

4 hard-boiled eggs

4 teaspoons truffle and porcini mushroom sauce or paste *(la truffata)*

about 1.5 litres hot Vegetable Stock (page 15) or Light Chicken Stock (page 16)

125 g unsalted butter

1 onion, finely chopped

400 g risotto rice

2–3 tablespoons chopped fresh flat leaf parsley

sea salt and freshly ground black pepper

parsley leaves, to serve

Serves 4

Cut the eggs in half and take out the yolks. Finely chop the whites. Mash the yolks in a small bowl with the truffle and mushroom sauce or paste.

Put the stock in a saucepan and keep at a gentle simmer. Melt half the butter in a large, heavy saucepan and add the onion. Cook gently for 10 minutes until soft, golden and translucent but not browned. Add the rice and stir until well coated with the butter and heated through.

Begin adding the stock, a large ladle at a time, stirring gently until each ladle has almost been absorbed by the rice. The risotto should be kept at a bare simmer throughout cooking, so don't let the rice dry out – add more stock as necessary. Continue until the rice is tender and creamy, but the grains still firm. (This should take 15–20 minutes depending on the type of rice used – check the packet instructions.)

Taste and season well with salt and pepper and beat in the remaining butter, truffled egg yolks, chopped egg whites and the parsley. Cover and let rest for a couple of minutes so the risotto can relax, then serve immediately. You may like to add a little more hot stock to the risotto just before you serve to loosen it, but don't let it wait around too long or the rice will turn mushy. Serve topped with the parsley leaves.

poultry and game

I couldn't resist this one – although it really is a French dish, it works so well with risotto. Confit chicken can be bought in cans if you can't be bothered to make it, but making your own is very satisfying and really incredibly easy. The duck fat or oil can be used over and over again if properly strained between each batch. Confit chicken is meltingly tender, and doesn't absorb fat or too much salt.

chicken confit risotto
risotto al pollo conservato

about 1.5 litres hot Light Chicken Stock (page 16)

125 g unsalted butter or 125 ml rendered duck fat or olive oil (listed below)

1 onion, finely chopped

3 garlic cloves, finely chopped

1 carrot, finely chopped

1 celery stalk, finely chopped

500 g risotto rice

50 g freshly grated Parmesan cheese

sea salt and freshly ground black pepper

chicken confit

4 chicken legs (thigh and drumstick joined) with skin on

3 tablespoons salt

3 garlic cloves, finely chopped

2 teaspoons chopped fresh thyme

2 bay leaves

about 600 ml olive oil or 500 g duck fat

Serves 4

To make the chicken confit, start the day before. Put the chicken legs in a non-reactive dish and rub with 3 tablespoons salt, garlic and thyme. Turn the legs skin side up and tuck in the bay leaves. Cover the dish with clingfilm and keep in the refrigerator overnight.

Remove the chicken from the refrigerator, rub off the excess salt and rinse under running water. Pat the legs dry with kitchen paper. Closely pack them in a single layer in a baking dish and cover with warmed olive oil or melted duck fat, making sure the legs are completely covered by the oil or fat. Cook in a preheated oven at 180°C (350°F) Gas 4 for about 45 minutes until cooked through. Set aside to cool completely in the oil or fat, then cover and refrigerate until needed. When ready to use, lift the chicken out of the oil or fat and wipe clean. Pull off the skin and take the meat from the bones and coarsely cut it up. Set aside.

Put the stock in a saucepan and keep at a gentle simmer. Heat half the butter (or duck fat or olive oil) in a large, heavy saucepan and add the onion, garlic, carrot and celery. Cook gently for 10 minutes until soft, golden and translucent but not browned. Add the rice and stir until well coated with the butter and heated through.

Begin adding the stock, a large ladle at a time, stirring gently until each ladle has almost been absorbed by the rice. The risotto should be kept at a bare simmer throughout cooking, so don't let the rice dry out – add more stock as necessary. Continue until the rice is tender and creamy, but the grains still firm. (This should take 15–20 minutes depending on the type of rice used – check the packet instructions.)

Taste and season well with salt and pepper and beat in the remaining butter and the Parmesan. Stir in the chicken and thyme. Cover and let rest for a couple of minutes so the risotto can relax and the chicken heat through, then serve immediately. You may like to add a little more hot stock to the risotto just before you serve to loosen it, but don't let it wait around too long or the rice will turn mushy.

My favourite cultivated mushrooms are the large, flat, open, almost black portobellos. They have much more flavour than younger ones with closed caps, and are almost the next best thing to wild mushrooms. They absorb a lot of butter and I like to get them really quite brown to concentrate the flavour. Tarragon goes particularly well with this combination, but can be overpowering, so don't use too much.

chicken and mushroom risotto
with tarragon
risotto al pollo, funghi e dragoncello

250 g large portobello mushrooms

150 g unsalted butter

1 garlic clove, finely chopped

about 1.5 litres hot Light Chicken Stock (page 16)

1 onion, finely chopped

1 celery stalk, finely chopped

600 g boneless, skinless chicken thighs and breast, chopped finely

500 g risotto rice

300 ml dry white wine

2 teaspoons chopped fresh tarragon

75 g freshly grated Parmesan cheese

sea salt and freshly ground black pepper

chopped fresh parsley, to serve

Serves 6

To prepare the mushrooms, cut them into long slices. Melt half the butter in a frying pan, add the mushrooms and garlic and fry over medium heat until browning at the edges. Transfer to a plate and set aside.

Put the stock in a saucepan and keep at a gentle simmer. Melt half the remaining butter in a large, heavy saucepan and add the onion and celery. Cook gently for 10 minutes until soft and golden but not browned. Add the chicken and cook for another 5 minutes, but do not let it colour and harden. Stir in the rice until well coated with butter, heated through and beginning to smell 'toasted'. Pour in the wine, bring to the boil and boil hard to reduce by half – this will concentrate the flavour and remove the raw taste of alcohol.

Begin adding the stock, a large ladle at a time, stirring gently until each ladle has been absorbed by the rice. The rice should always be at a gentle simmer. Continue in this way until the rice is tender and creamy, but the grains still firm. (This should take 15–20 minutes depending on the type of rice used – check the packet instructions.)

Taste and season well with salt and pepper and stir in the remaining butter, the tarragon and Parmesan. Cover and let rest for a couple of minutes to let the risotto relax. Reheat the mushrooms, then serve the risotto with the mushrooms piled on top, sprinkled with chopped parsley.

I first discovered the marriage of a little Vin Santo and chicken livers in Tuscany, when I was cooking a traditional topping of chicken livers for crostini. There wasn't an open bottle of wine handy, so I used a drop of Vin Santo. It was sublime. The sweet grapiness was perfect with chicken livers. Find the freshest, plumpest livers for this risotto.

chicken liver risotto
with vin santo
risotto ai fegatini e vin santo

175 g plump fresh chicken livers

about 1.5 litres hot Light Chicken Stock (page 16) or Vegetable Stock (page 15)

125 g unsalted butter

2 shallots, finely chopped

1 celery stalk, finely chopped

1 small carrot, finely chopped

3 tablespoons Italian Vin Santo or dry sherry

1 tablespoon sun-dried tomato paste or purée

400 g risotto rice, preferably vialone nano

2 tablespoons salted capers, rinsed and chopped

3 tablespoons chopped fresh parsley

sea salt and freshly ground black pepper

Serves 4

Trim any stringy bits from the livers with a sharp knife. Cut away any discoloured bits and cut into large (2 cm) pieces. Set aside.

Put the stock in a saucepan and keep at a gentle simmer. Melt half the butter in a large, heavy saucepan and add the shallots, celery and carrot. Cook gently for 6–8 minutes until soft, golden and translucent but not browned. Stir in the livers, then raise the heat until they are cooked and firm on the outside, soft and pink inside. Stir in the Vin Santo and tomato paste and boil hard until the liquid has all but evaporated. Add the rice and stir until well coated with the butter and vegetables and heated through.

Begin adding the stock, a large ladle at a time, stirring gently so as not to break up the chicken livers too much, until each ladle has almost been absorbed by the rice. The risotto should be kept at a bare simmer throughout cooking, so don't let the rice dry out – add more stock as necessary. Continue until the rice is tender and creamy, but the grains still firm. (This should take 15–20 minutes depending on the type of rice used – check the packet instructions.)

Taste and season well with salt and pepper and beat in the remaining butter, the capers and parsley. Cover and let rest for a couple of minutes so the risotto can relax, then serve immediately. You may like to add a little more hot stock to the risotto just before you serve to loosen it, but don't let it wait around too long or the rice will turn mushy.

Make this risotto really soupy, with vialone nano rice, as served in the Veneto – the land of lagoons and wildfowl. Wild duck would make all the difference to this dish if you have access to it, giving it a rich, gamey taste. The anchovies are barely perceptible in the risotto, but they add a deep, savoury flavour, which will make even the most domestic of ducks taste like game birds. The balsamic vinegar is my secret ingredient, again to give depth to the finished dish.

duck risotto with wilted spinach
risotto all'anatra con spinaci

about 1.5 litres hot Game Stock made with duck bones or Light Chicken Stock (page 16)

3 duck breasts with fat

125 g unsalted butter or the skin from the duck breasts

1 onion, finely chopped

2 garlic cloves, finely chopped

100 g pancetta, chopped

1 tablespoon chopped fresh sage

1 tablespoon chopped fresh rosemary

finely grated zest and juice of 1 unwaxed lemon

2 anchovies in salt, cleaned, or 4 anchovy fillets, rinsed and chopped

150 ml dry white wine (optional)

2 tablespoons balsamic vinegar

400 g risotto rice, such as vialone nano

200 g fresh young spinach, washed

sea salt and freshly ground black pepper

4 tablespoons freshly grated Parmesan cheese, to serve

Serves 4

Put the stock in a saucepan and keep at a gentle simmer. Pull the fat off the duck breasts and chop it. Chop the duck meat into small pieces. Melt half the butter (or use the duck fat and skin and slowly fry it in the pan for 5–10 minutes until the fat melts, then remove the solids) in a large, heavy saucepan and add the onion and garlic. Cook for 10 minutes over medium heat until soft and beginning to caramelize.

Add the duck, pancetta, sage, rosemary, lemon zest and anchovies and cook for 2–3 minutes until changing colour, but not browning. Pour in the wine and balsamic vinegar and boil hard for 1 minute to boil off the alcohol. Add 2 ladles of stock, cover and simmer very gently for 20 minutes or until the duck is tender. Stir in the rice, then begin adding the stock, a large ladle at a time, stirring gently until each ladle has almost been absorbed by the rice. The risotto should be kept at a bare simmer throughout cooking, so don't let the rice dry out – add more stock as necessary. Continue until the rice is tender and creamy, but the grains still firm. (This should take 15–20 minutes depending on the type of rice used – check the packet instructions.)

Taste and season well with salt, pepper and lemon juice, beat in the remaining butter, then stir in the spinach. Cover and let rest for a couple of minutes so the risotto can relax and the spinach wilt, then serve immediately. You may like to add a little more hot stock to the risotto just before you serve to loosen it, but don't let it wait around too long or the rice will turn mushy. Serve with freshly grated Parmesan cheese.

I was always excited when my father returned from a shoot with his game-bag full. Usually this meant pheasants, and this is one of the best ways to cook them. Roast pheasant is good too, but this is easier to eat and has all the wild, herby tastes of the hills.

pheasant and red wine risotto
risotto al fagiano e chianti

3 prepared pheasants or
6 boned pheasant breasts

about 1.5 litres hot Light Chicken
Stock or Game Stock (page 16)

2 bay leaves

125 g unsalted butter

1 onion, finely chopped

1 carrot, finely chopped

1 celery stalk, finely chopped

50 g pancetta, finely chopped

500 g risotto rice

300 ml red wine, such as Chianti

1 tablespoon chopped fresh thyme

75 g freshly grated Parmesan cheese

sea salt and freshly ground black pepper

chopped fresh parsley, to serve

Serves 6

Remove the breasts and legs from the pheasants and set aside. Cut up the carcass and add to the stock with the bay leaves. Simmer for 30 minutes before you start, then strain the stock into a pan and keep at simmering point on the top of the stove.

Pull the skin off the breasts and legs and cut the flesh into small pieces, discarding any bones. Melt half the butter in a large, heavy saucepan and add the onion, carrot and celery (this is a *soffritto*). Cook gently for 10 minutes until soft and golden but not browned. Add the pancetta and pheasant and cook for another 5 minutes, but do not let it brown and harden. Stir in the rice until well coated with butter, heated through and beginning to smell toasted. Pour in the wine, bring to the boil and boil hard to reduce by half – this will concentrate the flavour and remove the raw taste of alcohol.

Begin adding the stock, a large ladle at a time, stirring gently until each ladle has almost been absorbed by the rice. The risotto should be kept at a bare simmer throughout cooking, so don't let the rice dry out – add more stock as necessary. Continue until the rice is tender and creamy, but the grains still firm. (This should take 15–20 minutes depending on the type of rice used – check the packet instructions.)

Taste and season well with salt and pepper and stir in the remaining butter, the thyme and Parmesan. Cover and let rest for a couple of minutes so the risotto can relax, then serve immediately, sprinkled with chopped parsley.

This is a rich and earthy risotto, redolent of the hills of Tuscany or Umbria on an autumn day. Farm-reared rabbit is such good value, very tender with a better texture than chicken, but wild rabbit has more flavour. I use all the ingredients from the famous dish *Coniglio alla Cacciatora* in this risotto.

hunter's-style rabbit risotto
risotto con coniglio alla cacciatora

about 1.5 litres hot Light Chicken Stock (page 16) or Vegetable Stock (page 15)

125 g unsalted butter

1 onion, finely chopped

1 carrot, finely chopped

1 celery stalk, finely chopped

50 g speck or prosciutto, finely chopped

600 g boneless rabbit, cut into small cubes

500 g risotto rice

1 tablespoon tomato purée

150 ml red wine, such as Chianti

1 tablespoon chopped fresh rosemary

150 g chestnut mushrooms, quartered

50 g freshly grated Parmesan cheese

50 g Greek-style black olives, pitted and quartered

sea salt and freshly ground black pepper

sprigs of rosemary, to serve

Serves 6

Put the stock in a saucepan and keep at a gentle simmer. Melt half the butter in a large, heavy saucepan and add the onion, carrot and celery. Cook gently for 10 minutes until soft and golden but not browned. Add the speck or prosciutto and rabbit and cook for another 5 minutes, but do not let it colour and harden. Stir in the rice until well coated with butter, heated through and beginning to smell toasted. Mix the tomato purée with the wine and pour onto the rice. Bring to the boil and boil hard to reduce by half – this will concentrate the flavour and remove the raw taste of alcohol. Stir in the rosemary.

Begin adding the stock, a large ladle at a time, stirring gently until each ladle has almost been absorbed by the rice. The risotto should be kept at a bare simmer throughout cooking, so don't let the rice dry out – add more stock as necessary. Halfway through cooking, stir in the mushrooms, then continue cooking, adding stock until the rice is tender and creamy, but the grains still firm. (This should take 15–20 minutes depending on the type of rice used – check the packet instructions.)

Taste and season well with salt and pepper and stir in the remaining butter, the Parmesan and the olives. Cover and let rest for a couple of minutes so the risotto can relax, then serve immediately, topped with rosemary sprigs.

meat and bacon

A real rib-sticker for the winter months. This risotto originates in the Val d'Aosta on the Italian-French border, where the pork spareribs are usually just simmered in broth until tender. This may not appeal to all, so I have tossed them in olive oil and balsamic vinegar and grilled them until crisp. They are then served on top of the risotto made with broccoli. Try to use purple-sprouting broccoli or tenderstem, as these are both sweet and full of flavour. This is a great dish to eat casually with friends on a cold winter's night.

broccoli risotto with spareribs
risotto con broccoli a modo mio

Beef or Veal Stock (page 19) – see method

1 kg meaty pork spareribs, trimmed of any large amounts of fat

100 ml olive oil

3 tablespoons balsamic vinegar

risotto

300 g broccoli, trimmed and cut into 2.5 cm lengths or broken into florets

125 g unsalted butter

1 onion, finely chopped

400 g risotto rice

50 g freshly grated Parmesan cheese

sea salt and freshly ground black pepper

3 tablespoons chopped fresh sage leaves, to serve

about 1.5 litres stock (see method)

kitchen foil

Serves 4

Follow the recipe for Beef or Veal Stock on page 19, substituting the spareribs for the beef and bones, simmering for 2 hours and skimming often. Remove from the heat and lift out the spareribs. Chop up the ribs into manageable pieces. Put the oil and vinegar in a large bowl, whisk well, then add the ribs. Toss to coat, then set them in a foil-lined grill pan. Heat the grill and cook the spareribs for 10 minutes, turning and basting with the pan juices occasionally until browned and crisp. Keep them warm.

Strain the stock into a bowl through a colander lined with muslin and discard the contents of the colander. Reserve the stock – you should have about 1.5 litres. Return the stock to the pan and return to simmering point. Add the broccoli and cook for 6–8 minutes or until tender. Remove with a slotted spoon and set aside. Melt half the butter in a large, heavy saucepan and add the onion. Cook gently for 10 minutes until soft, golden and translucent but not browned. Add the rice and stir until well coated with the butter and heated through.

Begin adding the stock, a large ladle at a time, stirring gently until each ladle has almost been absorbed by the rice. The risotto should be kept at a bare simmer throughout cooking, so don't let the rice dry out – add more stock as necessary. Continue until the rice is tender and creamy, but the grains still firm. (This should take 15–20 minutes depending on the type of rice used – check the packet instructions.)

Taste and season well with salt and pepper, beat in the remaining butter and fold in the broccoli. Cover and let rest for a couple of minutes so the risotto can relax and the broccoli heat through. Serve immediately with the spareribs piled on top, sprinkled with chopped sage. You may like to add a little more hot stock to the risotto just before you serve to loosen it, but don't let it wait around too long or the rice will turn mushy.

Italian sausages are pure pork – nothing added except salt and pepper and maybe chilli or fennel seeds. They have a much better flavour than ordinary sausages, so it's worth seeking out a good Italian deli in your area. In Italy, you choose your cut of pork and the sausages are made in moments right in front of you, leaving you to choose your own seasonings. Luganega is the long, coiled sausage and, if not fresh, can be bought vacuum-packed or sometimes by mail order.

risotto with italian sausages and roasted onions

risotto con salsicce e cipolle arrostite

about 1.5 litres hot Light Chicken Stock (page 16) or Vegetable Stock (page 15)

125 g unsalted butter

500 g fresh Italian sausages, skins removed

1 onion, finely chopped

2 garlic cloves, finely chopped

150 ml Italian passata (strained crushed tomatoes)

2 teaspoons chopped fresh thyme

500 g risotto rice

75 g freshly grated Parmesan cheese, plus extra to serve

roasted onions

6 small whole red onions

100 ml olive oil

4 tablespoons balsamic vinegar

1 tablespoon chopped fresh thyme, plus extra sprigs to serve

sea salt and freshly ground black pepper

kitchen foil

Serves 6

To prepare the roasted onions, quarter them, then peel, keeping the root ends on to hold them together. Brush a roasting tin with a little olive oil and add the onions. Put the remaining olive oil, vinegar, thyme, salt and pepper in a bowl, whisk well, then brush over the onions, pouring any excess into the tin. Cover with foil and roast in a preheated oven at 200°C (400°F) Gas 6 for 15 minutes. Remove the foil and roast for 10 minutes or until nicely caramelized. Remove from the oven and keep them warm.

To make the risotto, put the stock in a saucepan and keep at a gentle simmer. Melt half the butter in a large, heavy saucepan and add the sausages. Cook over medium heat for 3–4 minutes, squashing with a spoon to break them up. Add the chopped onion and garlic and cook gently for 10 minutes until the onion is soft and golden. Add the passata and thyme and simmer for 5–10 minutes. Stir in the rice, making sure it is heated through before you add the stock.

Begin adding the stock, a large ladle at a time, stirring gently until each ladle has almost been absorbed by the rice. The risotto should be kept at a bare simmer throughout cooking, so don't let the rice dry out – add more stock as necessary. Continue until the rice is tender and creamy, but the grains still firm. (This should take 15–20 minutes depending on the type of rice used – check the packet instructions.)

Taste and season well with salt and pepper and beat in the remaining butter and all the Parmesan. Cover and let rest for a couple of minutes so the risotto can relax and the cheese melt. You may like to add a little more hot stock to the risotto just before you serve to loosen it, but don't let it wait around too long or the rice will turn mushy. Serve in warm bowls topped with the roasted onions and extra sprigs of thyme.

Once the staple food of the *gente di risaia* – the workers in the rice fields of Piemonte – this is a fantastic way to use any fresh beans in season. Although the quantity of salami used by the workers would have been small, I have used extra for a more affluent risotto. If you can't find fresh beans, use canned beans instead, and stir them in 5 minutes from the end of cooking to heat them through. Sometimes a glass of local Barolo would be added after the rice before the stock is added. This is a very soothing risotto.

salami and borlotti bean risotto

risotto con salame e fagioli borlotti

about 1.5 litres hot Beef or Veal Stock (page 19)

1 kg fresh borlotti beans (or similar) in the pod, shelled weight of 500 g

125 g unsalted butter

1 onion, finely chopped

150 g chunk of good salami, diced

400 g risotto rice, preferably carnaroli

75 g freshly grated Parmesan cheese, plus extra to serve

sea salt and freshly ground black pepper

Serves 6

Put the stock in a saucepan and keep at a gentle simmer. If using fresh beans, shell them and cook in the stock for about 20 minutes or until tender. Lift out with a slotted spoon and set aside.

Melt half the butter in a large, heavy saucepan and add the onion. Cook gently for 10 minutes until soft, golden and translucent but not browned. Stir in the salami and cook for 2 minutes. It must not brown. Add the rice and stir until well coated with the butter and heated through. Begin adding the stock, a large ladle at a time, stirring gently until each ladle has almost been absorbed by the rice. The risotto should be kept at a bare simmer throughout cooking, so don't let the rice dry out – add more stock as necessary. Continue until the rice is tender and creamy, but the grains still firm. (This should take 15–20 minutes depending on the type of rice used – check the packet instructions.) Stir in the beans just before the risotto is ready.

Taste and season well with salt and pepper and beat in the remaining butter and all the Parmesan cheese. Cover and let rest for a couple of minutes so the risotto can relax, then serve immediately. You may like to add a little more hot stock to the risotto just before you serve to loosen it, but don't let it wait around too long or the rice will turn mushy. Serve with extra grated Parmesan.

The leek is one of my favourite vegetables – it's not used enough in my opinion. Its sweet, delicate onion flavour is an excellent complement to salty cooked ham. Try to find ham sold in the piece so you can tear it into shreds – it will be more succulent than sliced ham. Roasting garlic softens and mellows the flavour until it is almost nutty.

ham and leek risotto
risotto con pancetta e porri

6 large garlic cloves

about 200 ml olive oil

500 g leeks

about 1.5 litres hot Light Chicken Stock (page 16)

500 g risotto rice

1 tablespoon coarsegrain mustard

350 g cold roasted ham, shredded

50 g freshly grated Parmesan cheese

sea salt and freshly ground black pepper

fried leeks

2 leeks

sunflower oil, for frying

Serves 4–6

Peel the garlic cloves and put them in a small saucepan. Cover with olive oil and heat to simmering. Simmer for about 20 minutes or until the garlic is golden and soft. Let cool in the oil.

To make the fried leeks, cut the 2 leeks into 7 cm lengths, then slice in half lengthways and cut into long, thin shreds. Fill a wok or large saucepan one-third full with the sunflower oil and heat to 175°C (350°F), add the shredded leeks and deep-fry for 1 minute until crisp and just golden. Lift out of the oil and drain on kitchen paper and set aside.

Slice the 500 g leeks (thinly or thickly, as you like) into rounds. Put the stock in a saucepan and keep at a gentle simmer. Heat 75 ml of the garlic-flavoured olive oil in a large, heavy saucepan. Add the leeks and sauté for a few minutes until beginning to soften and colour slightly, then stir in the garlic cloves. Pour in the rice and stir until well coated with oil and heated through.

Begin to add the simmering stock, a large ladle at a time, stirring until each ladle has been absorbed by the rice. Continue until the rice is tender and creamy, but the grains still firm. Stir in the mustard and ham. Season well, stir in the Parmesan, cover and let rest for a couple of minutes so the risotto can relax, before serving topped with a mound of fried leeks.

Here, a classic meat ragù is transformed into a creamy risotto. It is important not to brown the meat and vegetables too much – this will turn the meat into hard little bullets. It should brown just enough to turn from raw to cooked, then it will stay soft and homogenous. Cook the sauce very slowly, for as long as possible, 1–3 hours. The longer it simmers, the better it will taste. You can also make a big batch in a large covered casserole, then simmer it in the oven at 150°C (300°F) Gas 2 for 3 hours. Freeze what you don't use for later.

risotto with meat sauce
risotto al ragù

ragù

100 g unsalted butter

300 g lean beef, veal or pork mince

50 g speck or prosciutto with plenty of fat, minced or finely chopped

1 small onion, finely chopped

1 small carrot, finely chopped

1 celery stalk, finely chopped

3 tablespoons dry white wine

400 g tomato passata or puréed chopped tomatoes

1 tablespoon tomato purée

about 2 litres Beef or Veal Stock (page 19)

I bay leaf

sea salt and freshly ground black pepper

risotto

500 g risotto rice

75 g freshly grated Parmesan cheese, plus extra to serve

sea salt and freshly ground black pepper

Serves 6 generously

To make the ragù, melt half the butter in a heavy casserole over medium heat. Add the mince and speck or prosciutto, onion, carrot and celery. Brown very lightly (you are not trying to sear the meat, just turn it from pink to pale grey-brown). Make sure you break it up as it cooks so that there are no large lumps. Add the wine, turn up the heat and boil until evaporated. Turn the heat down again. Add the tomato passata and purée, mix well, then add 500 ml stock, the bay leaf, salt and pepper. Bring to the boil, stir well, then half-cover and turn the heat to a bare simmer. Simmer for about 2 hours or until the butter begins to separate on the surface: it should be rich and thick. Add salt and pepper to taste.

Set the remaining stock on the stove and keep at a gentle simmer. Stir the rice into the ragù, mixing well. Increase to a simmer. Begin adding the stock, a large ladle at a time, stirring gently until each ladle has almost been absorbed by the rice. The risotto should be kept at a bare simmer throughout cooking, so don't let the rice dry out – add more stock as necessary. Continue until the rice is tender and creamy, but the grains still firm, 15–20 minutes depending on the type of rice used (check the packet instructions).

Taste and season well with salt and pepper, remove the bay leaf and beat in the remaining butter and all the Parmesan. Cover and let rest for a couple of minutes so the risotto can relax and the cheese melt, then serve immediately. You may like to add a little more hot stock to the risotto just before you serve to loosen it, but don't let it wait around too long or the rice will turn mushy.

Artichokes are just made to go with lamb. Fresh smaller artichokes with a purple blush are best here, but you can use pared-down globe artichokes, the char-grilled ones sold in delis or even frozen artichoke bottoms or hearts. Canned artichokes are not so good.

risotto with lamb, artichokes, black olives and garlic

risotto con agnello, carciofi e olive nere

12 fresh artichokes*, or 12 char-grilled deli artichokes, or 8 frozen artichoke bottoms, thawed

butter, for frying (optional)

500 g lamb fillet, trimmed (or a really well-trimmed rack of lamb with no fat or gristle sticking to the bones)

1 tablespoon olive oil

about 1.5 litres hot Light Chicken Stock (page 16), Beef or Veal Stock (page 19) or Vegetable Stock (page 15)

125 g unsalted butter

2 shallots, finely chopped

1 celery stalk, finely chopped

1 small carrot, finely chopped

6 roasted garlic cloves (see Roasted Garlic Risotto with Goats' Cheese and Rosemary on page 72)

400 g risotto rice

150 ml fruity white wine

sea salt and freshly ground black pepper

to serve

20 Greek-style black olives (the dark wrinkled ones), pitted but left as large as possible

1 tablespoon finely chopped fresh marjoram

Serves 4

*To prepare fresh young artichokes, see page 45.

First prepare the fresh artichokes, if using. Brush with olive oil and char-grill for 5 minutes on a stove-top grill pan, turning often. Otherwise, quarter the bought char-grilled ones and set aside, or slice the thawed artichoke bottoms and fry in a little butter until golden.

Preheat the oven to 220°C (425°F) Gas 7. Heat an ovenproof frying pan until very hot. Season the lamb well. Add the oil to the pan, then the lamb and a tablespoon of the butter and cook over high heat for 2–3 minutes until well browned on all sides. Put the pan straight into the oven and roast for 7–12 minutes for the fillet (12–20 minutes for the rack), depending on how rare you like your meat. When cooked, lift out the lamb onto a heated plate, cover and let it relax in a warm place while you make the risotto. Pour a ladle of the stock into the pan and deglaze, scraping up all the sediment. Set aside.

Put the stock in a saucepan and keep at a gentle simmer. Melt half the remaining butter in a large, heavy saucepan and add the shallots, celery, carrot and roasted garlic cloves. Cook gently for 10 minutes until soft, golden and translucent but not browned. Add the rice and stir until well coated with the butter and heated through. Pour in the wine and boil hard until it has reduced and almost disappeared. This will remove the taste of raw alcohol.

Add the pan juices from cooking the lamb, then begin adding the stock, a large ladle at a time, stirring gently until each ladle has almost been absorbed by the rice. The risotto should be kept at a bare simmer throughout cooking, so don't let the rice dry out – add more stock as necessary. Continue until the rice is tender and creamy, but the grains still firm. (This should take 15–20 minutes depending on the type of rice used – check the packet instructions.)

Stir in the olives and marjoram, taste and season well with salt and pepper and beat in all the remaining butter. Fold in the artichokes. Cover and let rest for a couple of minutes so the risotto can relax. Carve the meat into thick slices, then serve the risotto immediately, topped with the sliced lamb. You may like to add a little more hot stock to the risotto just before you serve to loosen it, but don't let the risotto wait around too long or the rice will turn mushy.

fish and seafood

One of my favourite risottos, this is stunning to look at. I love the rich iodine taste the ink gives to the sauce, and the sweetness of the squid or cuttlefish. Cleaned squid is available from most fishmongers. The all-important ink sacs have been packaged into little plastic sachets — find them in the chiller cabinets at fishmongers and some delis. Using a cuttlefish will give immense satisfaction and a stronger flavour to the risotto. Just for interest, *seppie* are cuttlefish, *calamari* are squid.

black risotto
risotto al nero di seppie

3 tablespoons extra virgin olive oil

½ onion, finely chopped

1 garlic clove, finely chopped

600 g cleaned squid plus two sachets squid ink or 900 g whole cuttlefish (see below)

about 1.5 litres hot Fish Stock (page 20)

150 ml dry white wine

500 g risotto rice, preferably vialone nano

50 g unsalted butter, softened

2 tablespoon grappa (optional)

3 tablespoons finely chopped fresh flat leaf parsley

sea salt and freshly ground black pepper

freshly grated Parmesan cheese, to serve (optional)

Serves 4–6

If using squid, cut body and tentacles into thin rings and small pieces. Keep some of the tentacles whole if you like. Heat the oil in a saucepan and add the onion and garlic. Cook gently for 10 minutes until soft, golden and translucent but not browned. Add the squid, 2 ladles of stock and the wine, then cover and cook gently for about 20 minutes or until tender, adding a little stock to the pan if necessary during cooking.

Add the rice and stir until well coated with the squid mixture and heated through. Mix the ink with a little stock and stir into the risotto. Begin adding the stock, a large ladle at a time, stirring gently until each ladle has almost been absorbed by the rice. The risotto should be kept at a bare simmer throughout cooking, so don't let the rice dry out — add more stock as necessary. Continue until the rice is tender and creamy and very *all'ondo* (liquid like a wave) but the grains still firm. (This should take 15–20 minutes depending on the type of rice used — check the packet instructions.)

Taste and season well with salt and pepper and beat in the butter and grappa, if using. Cover and let rest for a couple of minutes so the risotto can relax, then serve immediately topped with the chopped parsley, together with a bowl of Parmesan, if using.

Note To prepare fresh cuttlefish or squid, rinse it, then pull the tentacles and head away from the body. Carefully remove the silvery ink sacs from the heads without piercing them. Cut off all the internal organs still attached to the head. Put the ink sacs in a tea strainer over a small bowl and press out the ink with the back of a spoon. Cut through the thin skin covering the cuttlefish bone in the body and lift the bone out. Wash everything thoroughly in cold water and cut the body and tentacles into thin rings and small squares.

For those who aren't brave enough to try *risotto nero*, made with squid ink, but still love squid, then this is for you. There is no sign of ink, just squid, garlic, wine and parsley. You can make this with fresh or frozen prepared squid. If you have the tentacles, they make a great topping – just quickly sear them on a stove-top grill pan. I sometimes fry a little extra sliced garlic and chopped red chilli in olive oil and pour this over the risotto before serving.

white squid risotto
risotto bianco con calamari

about 1.5 litres hot Light Chicken Stock (page 16) or Vegetable Stock (page 15)

300 g fresh or frozen prepared squid (to prepare fresh squid or cuttlefish, see page 107)

125 g unsalted butter

1 onion or 2 shallots, finely chopped

2–3 large garlic cloves, finely chopped

75 ml dry white wine

300 g risotto rice, preferably carnaroli

2 tablespoons chopped fresh parsley

1–2 tablespoons olive oil

sea salt and freshly ground black pepper

a stove-top grill pan or frying pan

Serves 4

Put the stock in a saucepan and keep at a gentle simmer. Cut the squid into rings or small pieces and reserve the tentacles, if using. Melt half the butter in a large, heavy saucepan and add the onion or shallots and the garlic. Cook gently for 5 minutes until translucent but not browned. Add the squid, then the wine and cook gently for 5 minutes, until the squid is white and the wine beginning to disappear. Add the rice and stir until well coated with the butter, wine and squid and heated through.

Begin adding the stock, a large ladle at a time, stirring gently until each ladle has almost been absorbed by the rice. The risotto should be kept at a bare simmer throughout cooking, so don't let the rice dry out – add more stock as necessary. Continue until the rice is tender and creamy, but the grains still firm. (This should take 15–20 minutes depending on the type of rice used – check the packet instructions.)

Taste and season well with salt and pepper and beat in the remaining butter and the parsley. Cover and let rest for a couple of minutes so the risotto can relax. Meanwhile heat a stove-top grill pan to smoking hot, toss the tentacles in the olive oil to coat and add them to the pan. Cook for 1–2 minutes, then remove to a plate. Check the risotto – you may like to add a little more hot stock to the risotto just before you serve to loosen it, but don't let it wait around too long or the rice will turn mushy. Serve with the tentacles on top.

Make this risotto with whatever seafood you can find, but make it as varied as possible. Cooking the seafood in the stock before making the risotto will intensify its flavour. Italians do not generally serve grated Parmesan with seafood, so don't ask for any in a restaurant – it may be frowned on.

seafood risotto
risotto ai frutti di mare

375 g uncooked shell-on prawns

1.5 litres hot Fish Stock or Quick Seafood Stock (page 20)

6 baby squid, cleaned

6 fresh scallops

600 g fresh mussels

300 g small fresh clams

75 g unsalted butter

1 onion, finely chopped

500 g risotto rice, preferably carnaroli

300 ml dry white wine

sea salt and freshly ground black pepper

3 tablespoons chopped fresh parsley, to serve

Serves 6 generously

Pull off the prawn heads and put them in the stock with the wine, bring to the boil, cover and simmer for 20 minutes. Cut the squid into rings and trim the tentacles. Remove the hard white muscle from the side of each scallop and separate the white flesh from the orange coral. Scrub the mussels well and pull off any beards. Discard broken ones and any that don't close when sharply tapped against a work surface. Rinse the clams well.

Strain the stock into a clean pan and heat to simmering point. Add the prawns and cook for 2 minutes. Add the squid, scallops and corals and cook for a further 2 minutes. Remove them all with a slotted spoon and set aside. Put the mussels and clams into the stock and bring to the boil. Cover and cook for 5 minutes or until all the shellfish have opened. Remove with a slotted spoon and set aside. This will remove the raw taste of alcohol.

Melt the butter in a large, heavy saucepan and add the onion. Cook gently for 10 minutes until softened but not browned. Pour in the rice and stir until well coated with butter and heated through. Add the wine and bring to the boil. Boil fast until reduced by half.

Begin to add the hot stock, a large ladle at a time, stirring until each ladle has been absorbed by the rice. Continue until all but 2 ladles of stock are left, and the rice is tender but still has some bite to it, 15–20 minutes.

Taste and season well with salt and pepper. Finally stir in the remaining stock and all the seafood and cook gently with the lid on for 5 minutes or until hot. The risotto shouldn't be too thick. Transfer to a large warmed bowl and sprinkle with the parsley. Serve immediately.

Crab makes a delicious risotto, especially when speckled with red chilli. Although fresh crab is preferable, it's a bit fiddly to prepare and fishmongers sell frozen white and dark crabmeat which is very acceptable for this recipe. I like to stir in the creamy dark meat at the end, but this may not be to all tastes. Serve topped with crab claws.

crab and chilli risotto
risotto al granchio e peperoncino

about 1.5 litres hot Quick Seafood Stock, Fish Stock (page 20) or Vegetable Stock (page 15)

100 g unsalted butter

3 shallots, finely chopped

2 celery stalks, finely chopped

400 g risotto rice

1 fresh red chilli, deseeded and finely chopped

1 bay leaf

150 ml dry white wine

250 g fresh white crabmeat (or frozen and thawed)

sea salt and freshly ground black pepper

to serve

4–8 meaty crab claws, cooked and cracked

4 tablespoons chopped fresh flat leaf parsley

Serves 4

Put the stock in a saucepan and keep at a gentle simmer. Melt half the butter in a large, heavy saucepan and add the shallots and celery. Cook gently for 5–7 minutes until soft, golden and translucent but not browned. Add the rice, chilli and bay leaf, stir until well coated with the butter, translucent and heated through. Pour in the wine and boil hard until it has reduced and almost disappeared. This will remove the taste of raw alcohol.

Begin adding the stock, a large ladle at a time, stirring gently until each ladle has almost been absorbed by the rice. The risotto should be kept at a bare simmer throughout cooking, so don't let the rice dry out – add more stock as necessary. Continue until the rice is tender and creamy, but the grains still firm. (This should take 15–20 minutes depending on the type of rice used – check the packet instructions.)

Five minutes before the rice is ready, stir in half the crabmeat. When the rice is cooked, taste and season well with salt and pepper and stir in the remaining butter. Remove the bay leaf. Fold in the remaining crabmeat, being careful not to break up any lumps. Cover and let rest for a couple of minutes so the risotto can relax, then serve immediately. Serve topped with the crab claws and lots of chopped fresh parsley.

This is a quick way to cook a special risotto. Adding pounded shells of the lobster to a vegetable stock will improve the flavour. If making this with prawns or scampi, cook them first, peel them, then pound the shells and add to the stock. Add the chopped prawn or scampi tails where you would the lobster flesh.

lobster, prawn or scampi risotto
risotto all'aragosta o gamberi o scampi

about 1.5 litres hot Quick Seafood Stock (page 20) or Vegetable Stock (page 15)

2 medium cooked lobsters, about 500–600 g each, or similar weight of prawns or scampi

125 g unsalted butter

2 shallots, finely chopped

500 g risotto rice

3 tablespoons sweet red vermouth

sea salt and freshly ground black pepper

fresh lemon juice

a pinch of cayenne, to serve

Serves 6

Put the stock in a saucepan and keep at a gentle simmer. Split the lobsters in half and remove the stomach sac and long intestine. Prise out the tail meat and any red coral or roe and set aside. Crack the claws and extract the meat and set aside. Put all the shells including the heads into a solid bowl and pound them with the end of a rolling pin until they are broken into small fragments. Add these to the stock and simmer for 30 minutes. Cut the lobster meat into chunks and chop up the roe. Strain the stock through a fine sieve and return to the heat. Discard the contents of the strainer.

Melt half the butter in a large, heavy saucepan and add the shallots. Cook gently for 5 minutes until soft, golden and translucent but not browned. Add the rice and stir until well coated with the butter and heated through. Pour in the vermouth and boil hard until it has reduced and almost disappeared. This will remove the taste of raw alcohol.

Begin adding the stock, a large ladle at a time, stirring gently until each ladle has almost been absorbed by the rice. The risotto should be kept at a bare simmer throughout cooking, so don't let the rice dry out – add more stock as necessary. Continue until the rice is tender and creamy, but the grains still firm. (This should take 15–20 minutes depending on the type of rice used – check the packet instructions.)

Taste and season well with salt, pepper and lemon juice, beat in the remaining butter and reserved roe and gently fold in the lobster meat. Cover and let rest for a couple of minutes so the risotto can relax and the lobster heat through, then serve immediately. You may like to add a little more hot stock to the risotto just before you serve to loosen it, but don't let it wait around too long or the rice will turn mushy. Serve sprinkled with a little cayenne.

Cooking this rich risotto with dry vermouth instead of wine gives it a certain finesse and a herbal note. I often use a little dry vermouth when cooking fish and seafood when I don't have any wine open.

scallop and spring onion risotto
risotto con capesante e cipollotti

about 1.5 litres hot Quick Seafood Stock, Fish Stock (page 20) or Vegetable Stock (page 15)

12 large fresh or frozen scallops (with or without orange roes or coral)

125 g unsalted butter

6 spring onions, sliced or chopped – white and green parts kept separate

400 g risotto rice, preferably carnaroli

75 ml dry white vermouth

sea salt and freshly ground black pepper

Serves 4

Put the stock in a saucepan and keep at a gentle simmer. Look at the scallops and check to see if there is a tiny tough white muscle clinging to the side – if there is, pull off and discard. Separate the corals or roes from the white meat. Slice each scallop in half around the middle. Set aside. Melt half the butter in a large, heavy saucepan and, when foaming, fry the scallops quickly, browning them on both sides. Remove to a plate before they overcook: they will only take 2 minutes at the most. Add the white part of the spring onion and cook gently for 3–4 minutes until soft, golden and translucent but not browned.

Add the rice and stir until well coated with the butter and heated through. Pour in the vermouth and boil hard until it has reduced and almost disappeared. This will remove the taste of raw alcohol.

Begin adding the stock, a large ladle at a time, stirring gently until each ladle has almost been absorbed by the rice. The risotto should be kept at a bare simmer throughout cooking, so don't let the rice dry out – add more stock as necessary. Continue until the rice is tender and creamy, but the grains still firm. (This should take 15–20 minutes depending on the type of rice used – check the packet instructions.)

Taste and season well with salt and pepper, beat in the remaining butter and fold in the scallops and green parts of the spring onions. Cover and let rest for a couple of minutes so the risotto can relax and the scallops heat through, then serve immediately. You may like to add a little more hot stock to the risotto just before you serve to loosen it, but don't let it wait around too long or the rice will turn mushy and the scallops will overcook.

Though it still tastes luxurious, the ingredients for this risotto are ordinary storecupboard ingredients. Canned smoked fish is a wonderful standby – for extra flavour, keep the oil and use it instead of the butter for softening the vegetables. A hint of tarragon is always good with smoky things, as is the sweetness of the leeks. This would also work well with flakes of any smoked fish such as mackerel or Scottish 'smokies' (smoked haddock).

smoked mussel or oyster and leek risotto

risotto con cozze o ostriche affumicate

about 1.5 litres hot Vegetable Stock (page 15)

125 g unsalted butter

1 large leek, finely sliced or chopped (all the white part and half of the green)

1 celery stalk, finely chopped

400 g risotto rice, preferably carnaroli

75 ml dry white vermouth

1 teaspoon chopped fresh tarragon

3 cans smoked mussels or oysters, 85 g each, drained

sea salt and freshly ground black pepper

Serves 4

Put the stock in a saucepan and keep at a gentle simmer. Melt half the butter in a large, heavy saucepan and, when foaming, add the sliced leek and celery and cook gently for 5 minutes until softened but not browned. Add the rice and stir until well coated with the butter and heated through. Pour in the vermouth and boil hard until it has reduced and almost disappeared. This will remove the taste of raw alcohol. Add the tarragon.

Begin adding the stock, a large ladle at a time, stirring gently until each ladle has almost been absorbed by the rice. The risotto should be kept at a bare simmer throughout cooking, so don't let the rice dry out – add more stock as necessary. Continue until the rice is tender and creamy, but the grains still firm. (This should take 15–20 minutes depending on the type of rice used – check the packet instructions.)

Taste and season well with salt and pepper, beat in the remaining butter and fold in the smoked mussels or oysters. Cover and let rest for a couple of minutes so the risotto can relax and the seafood heat through, then serve immediately. You may like to add a little more hot stock to the risotto just before you serve to loosen it, but don't let it wait around too long or the rice will turn mushy and the seafood will overcook.

A simple risotto relying on the freshness and delicate flavours of the mussels or clams. The smaller mussels or clams are always the sweetest, so choose them instead of big fat ones. The secret here is not to overcook them, so steam them until they JUST open, then strain immediately. Try to strain the resulting cooking liquid through a fine tea strainer or muslin, because clams and mussels can be gritty. When I have it, I like to add chopped fresh chervil, which gives a hint of aniseed. This should be quite a loose risotto.

mussel or clam risotto
risotto con cozze o vongole

1.5 kg live mussels or small clams

about 1.5 litres hot Fish Stock (page 20)
or Vegetable Stock (page 15)

125 g unsalted butter

1 small onion, finely chopped

2 garlic cloves, finely chopped

500 g risotto rice, preferably vialone nano

3 tablespoons chopped fresh flat leaf parsley

sea salt and freshly ground black pepper

Serves 6

Discard any mussels or clams with broken shells, or any that are open and will not close when sharply tapped against a surface. Wash and scrub them thoroughly, pulling off any beards, then let soak in cold water for an hour to purge them. Drain and transfer to a large saucepan over high heat, with no extra water other than whatever is still clinging to them. Cover and steam for 2–5 minutes (2–3 for clams, 4–5 for mussels), until they open fully, giving the pan a shake now and then. Strain them through a colander and reserve the cooking liquid. When cool enough to handle, remove the flesh from the shells, leaving a few in the shell for serving. Strain the resulting liquid through a very fine sieve or muslin.

Put the stock in a saucepan and keep at a gentle simmer. Melt half the butter in a large, heavy saucepan and add the onion and garlic. Cook gently for 10 minutes until soft, golden and translucent but not browned. Add the rice and stir until well coated with the butter and heated through. Stir in the strained mussel liquid. When this has been absorbed, begin adding the stock, a large ladle at a time, stirring gently until each ladle has almost been absorbed by the rice. The risotto should be kept at a bare simmer throughout cooking, so don't let the rice dry out – add more stock as necessary. Continue until the rice is tender and creamy, but the grains still firm. (This should take 15–20 minutes depending on the type of rice used – check the packet instructions.)

Taste and season well with salt and pepper, beat in the remaining butter and gently fold in the cooked mussels or clams and 2 tablespoons of the parsley. Cover and let rest for a few minutes so the risotto can relax and the shellfish heat through, then serve immediately topped with the remaining parsley and the reserved mussels in their shells. You may like to add a little more hot stock to the risotto just before you serve to loosen it, but don't let it wait around too long or the rice will turn mushy.

The fresh and slightly musky flavour of caper is delicious in a fish risotto, especially if they are the salted ones, which are more pungent than those in vinegar. The tuna is cut thicker than normal by Italian standards and grilled until crusty on the outside, but pink and tender inside. Masked with a fresh, vibrant sauce from Sicily, this is perfect for a summer meal.

caper risotto with grilled tuna and salmoriglio sauce

risotto con capperi, tonno e salmoriglio

4 tuna steaks, cut 2.5 cm thick

6 tablespoons extra virgin olive oil

sea salt and freshly ground black pepper

salmoriglio sauce

finely grated zest and juice of
½ large unwaxed lemon, or to taste

a pinch of sugar

4 tablespoons extra virgin olive oil

1 garlic clove, finely chopped

2 teaspoons dried oregano

2 tablespoons fresh mint, finely chopped

caper risotto

about 1.5 litres hot Fish Stock (page 20)
or Vegetable Stock (page 15)

1 onion, finely chopped

500 g risotto rice

150 ml dry white wine

4 tablespoons capers in salt, rinsed,
then soaked for 10 minutes in warm water

finely grated zest and juice of
1 unwaxed lemon, to taste

sea salt and freshly ground black pepper

kitchen foil

Serves 4

To make the salmoriglio sauce, put the lemon juice and sugar in a bowl, stir to dissolve, then add the lemon zest. Whisk in the 4 tablespoons olive oil, then stir in the garlic, oregano and chopped mint. Set aside to infuse.

Preheat the grill or barbecue. Brush the tuna with 2 tablespoons olive oil and season with salt and pepper. Set on a rack in a foil-lined grill pan. Grill or barbecue for about 1–2 minutes on each side until crusty on the outside and still pink in the middle. Remove from the heat, cover and keep it warm while you make the risotto.

Put the stock in a saucepan and keep at a gentle simmer. Heat 4 tablespoons olive oil in a large, heavy saucepan and add the onion. Cook gently for 10 minutes until soft, golden and translucent but not browned. Add the rice and stir until well coated with the oil and heated through. Add the wine and boil hard until it has reduced and almost disappeared. This will remove the taste of raw alcohol.

Begin adding the stock, a large ladle at a time, stirring gently until each ladle has almost been absorbed by the rice. The risotto should be kept at a bare simmer throughout cooking, so don't let the rice dry out – add more stock as necessary. Continue until the rice is tender and creamy, but the grains still firm. (This should take 15–20 minutes depending on the type of rice used – check the packet instructions.)

Taste and season well with salt and pepper, chopped capers, lemon juice and zest to taste. Cover and let rest for a couple of minutes so the risotto can relax. You may like to add a little more hot stock to the risotto just before you serve to loosen it, but don't let it wait around too long or the rice will turn mushy. Slice the tuna steaks. Spoon the risotto onto warm plates and set the sliced tuna on top of each. Spoon the sauce over the top and serve immediately.

Smoked salmon has become very fashionable in Italy and I have even seen it on pizzas – overcooked and not very pleasant. However, smoked salmon is sublime in a very creamy risotto enriched with butter, cream and Parmesan (one of the few times it is respectable to use Parmesan in a fish or seafood risotto). This risotto should be quite liquid.

smoked salmon risotto
risotto cremoso con salmone affumicato

about 1.5 litres hot Fish Stock (page 20) or Vegetable Stock (page 15)

125 g unsalted butter

3 shallots, very finely chopped

1 garlic clove, finely chopped

300 g risotto rice

75 ml dry vermouth

4 tablespoons double cream or 2 tablespoons mascarpone cheese

50 g finely grated Parmesan cheese, plus extra to serve

200 g sliced smoked salmon, cut into thin strips

2 tablespoons chopped fresh dill

finely grated zest and juice of 1 unwaxed lemon

sea salt and freshly ground black pepper

Serves 4

Put the stock in a saucepan and keep at a gentle simmer. Melt half the butter in a large, heavy saucepan and add the shallots and garlic. Cook gently for 10 minutes until soft, golden and translucent but not browned. Add the rice and stir until well coated with the butter and heated through. Pour in the vermouth and boil hard until it has reduced and almost disappeared. This will remove the taste of raw alcohol.

Begin adding the stock, a large ladle at a time, stirring gently until each ladle has almost been absorbed by the rice. The risotto should be kept at a bare simmer throughout cooking, so don't let the rice dry out – add more stock as necessary. Continue until the rice is tender and creamy, but the grains still firm. (This should take 15–20 minutes depending on the type of rice used – check the packet instructions.)

Taste and season well with salt and pepper and beat in the remaining butter, the cream and Parmesan. Gently fold in half the salmon, and all the dill and lemon zest. Cover and let rest for a couple of minutes so the risotto can relax and the flavours develop. Taste again and season with lemon juice, then serve immediately. You may like to add a little more hot stock to the risotto just before you serve to loosen it, but don't let it wait around too long or the rice will turn mushy. Top with the remaining smoked salmon.

other ways with risotto

Barlotto is one of my friend Nick Nairn's specialities. He loves to make this in autumn after mushroom-hunting near his cooking school on the Lake of Menteith in Scotland. I have always loved the chewy nuttiness of this recipe, and thought the title was a bit of a pun on the words barley and risotto, but have recently found out that a similar dish is made in Venezia-Friuli-Giulia called *orzotto*. To make serving this dish easier, Nick suggests making the barlotto in advance and reheating it – something it does well, because unlike rice, barley doesn't go soggy with keeping.

barlotto with red wine and mushrooms

orzotto al vino rosso e funghi

3 tablespoons olive oil

175 g pearl barley, washed and drained

1 small onion, finely chopped

1 garlic clove, finely chopped

500 ml hot Light Chicken Stock (page 16), Vegetable Stock (page 15) or water

1 tablespoon light soy sauce

150 ml red wine

300 g fresh chanterelles (or other wild and cultivated mushrooms, such as porcini or portobellos)

75 g unsalted butter

2 tablespoons chopped fresh parsley

1 tablespoon chopped fresh tarragon

sea salt and freshly ground black pepper

kitchen foil

Serves 4

Heat the oil in a large saucepan, then add the barley and stir until it starts to turn golden (not brown) – this will take about 5 minutes. Add the onion and garlic and continue frying until the barley starts to brown, 5–10 minutes. Don't let it burn, but you want a good, toasted flavour.

Add the stock, soy sauce, red wine, salt and pepper. Bring to the boil, turn down the heat, part-cover with a lid, then simmer gently until nearly all the liquid has been absorbed – this should take at least 30 minutes. The beauty of this one is that you don't need to stir it constantly.

Meanwhile, brush or scrape the mushrooms clean (slicing any bigger ones to size) and heat a frying pan until hot. Add 50 g of the butter and all the mushrooms. Stir-fry over medium heat until lightly browned, 4–5 minutes. Season with salt and pepper. Add the stir-fried mushrooms to the barley and mix gently. Remove from the heat and cover with kitchen foil with a few holes pierced in it to let the barley swell and absorb all the liquid. Leave it in a warm place for 15 minutes. (At this stage, you could let the barlotto cool, reheating it for serving up to 24 hours later.)

To serve, put the barlotto pan back on the heat and beat in the parsley, tarragon and the remaining 25 g of butter. Stir well until hot, add salt and pepper to taste and pile onto heated plates. Serve immediately.

Supplì are real comfort food. When you bite one, you can pull the melted oozing mozzarella into strings that are said to look like telephone wires strung from pole to pole – hence the name, *supplì al telefono*. You can make it with leftover risotto, but it is so good (kids adore it), it is worth making from scratch as a starter or a snack.

rice croquettes with tomato sauce
supplì al telefono con sugo di pomodoro

tomato sauce

125 ml olive oil

2 garlic cloves, chopped

1 teaspoon dried (not fresh) oregano

800 g fresh tomatoes, skinned and coarsely chopped, or 800 g canned chopped tomatoes

sea salt and freshly ground black pepper

supplì

2 eggs, lightly beaten

⅓ recipe Parmesan and Butter Risotto (page 63)

100 g mozzarella cheese, cut into 20 cubes

2 slices of cooked ham or mortadella, cut into 20 strips

100 g dried white breadcrumbs, for coating

sea salt and freshly ground black pepper

oil, for deep-frying

Makes 20

To make the tomato sauce, heat the oil almost to smoking point in a large shallow pan or wok. Standing back (it will splutter if it's at the right temperature), add the garlic, oregano, tomatoes and pepper. To acquire its distinctive, concentrated, almost caramelized flavour, the tomatoes must fry at a very lively heat in a shallow pan, so cook over fierce heat for 5-8 minutes or until the sauce is thick and glossy. Add salt to taste, pass through a food mill or blend in a food processor, then sieve to remove the seeds. Set aside.

Beat the eggs into the risotto. Spread the mixture out on a plate and let cool completely, about 1 hour.

Take a large spoonful of risotto and, with damp hands, mould it into an egg shape. Insert your little finger down through the top of the egg but not quite to the bottom, to make a hole inside. Push in a cube of cheese wrapped with a strip of ham and pinch the top over to seal. Roll the egg shape into a fat cylinder, making sure the filling doesn't burst through. Set on a tray while you make the others. Put the breadcrumbs in a shallow bowl. Roll the *supplì* in the breadcrumbs until evenly coated. At this stage they can be covered and left in the refrigerator for up to 1 day.

Heat the oil in a large saucepan until a crumb will sizzle immediately – 180°C (350°F). Fry 3–4 at a time for 4–5 minutes until deep golden. Drain on kitchen paper, sprinkle with salt and serve immediately with warm tomato sauce (or keep warm in a low oven for up to 15 minutes).

These little, cocktail-sized mouthfuls will mysteriously jump into your mouth as you cook them. After they are completely assembled, they can be refrigerated for up to a day, ready to fry at the last moment. They will keep warm in a low oven for 30 minutes – but keep them covered and don't add a topping until the last minute. Deep-fried basil leaves are crisply translucent and make a beautiful topping. To cook them, heat oil in a deep-fryer to 190°C (375°F). Make sure the basil leaves are dry, then put into the basket. Fry for 30 seconds – they will hiss alarmingly. Remove immediately and drain on kitchen paper. They will crisp more on cooling.

little tomato risotto cakes
saltimbocca di risotto

500 ml Vegetable Stock (page 15)

500 ml tomato juice or mixed vegetable juice, such as V8

3 tablespoons olive oil

1 small onion, finely chopped

1 garlic clove, finely chopped

225 g risotto rice, preferably arborio

150 ml dry white wine

4 tablespoons sun-dried tomato paste

125 g mi-cuit or sun-blushed tomatoes, chopped

50 g freshly grated Parmesan cheese

1 small egg, beaten

32 fresh basil leaves, plus extra to serve

16 paperthin slices of pancetta, halved

sea salt and freshly ground black pepper

Makes about 32

Put the stock and tomato or vegetable juice in a saucepan and keep at a gentle simmer. Heat the olive oil in a large, heavy saucepan and add the onion. Cook gently for 5 minutes, then add the garlic and cook for a further 5 minutes until soft, golden and translucent but not browned. Add the rice, then stir until well coated with the oil and heated through. Pour in the wine and boil hard until it has reduced and almost disappeared. This will remove the taste of raw alcohol. Stir in the sun-dried tomato paste.

Add the stock, a large ladle at a time, stirring gently until each ladle has almost been absorbed by the rice. The risotto should be kept at a bare simmer throughout cooking, so don't let the rice dry out – add more stock as necessary. Continue until the rice is tender and creamy, and thicker than normal. (This should take about 20 minutes depending on the type of rice used – check the packet instructions.) Stir in the sun-blushed tomatoes and Parmesan.

Taste and season well with salt and pepper, then beat in the egg. Spread out the mixture on a tray until cool enough to handle, about 30 minutes. Roll into bite-sized balls with damp hands, flatten, set on a tray and cover with clingfilm. Leave to firm up in the refrigerator. When firm, put a basil leaf on top of each one and wrap with a strip of pancetta. Heat a little oil in a non-stick frying pan and fry for about 1 minute on each side until golden. Serve warm, topped with fresh or quickly deep-fried basil leaves (see recipe introduction).

These crisp golden balls, stuffed with leftover meat ragù, are eaten as street food in Sicily. However, when made cocktail snack size, they are perfect to serve with drinks. Unlike making a true risotto, you should overcook the rice to make it really stick together. The mixture should be very thick before it is cooled and can be made with leftover risotto.

arancine di riso

75 g unsalted butter

1 onion, finely chopped

150 ml dry white wine

275 g risotto rice, preferably arborio

900 ml hot Vegetable Stock (page 15) or Light Chicken Stock (page 16)

8 saffron threads or ¼ teaspoon powdered saffron

25 g freshly grated Parmesan cheese

1 small egg

about 250 g meat ragù (page 101), or use leftover ragù

sea salt and freshly ground black pepper

oil, for deep-frying

coating

100 g plain flour

2 large eggs, beaten

125 g dried white breadcrumbs

an electric deep-fryer or wok

Serves 4–6

Melt the butter in a large, heavy saucepan and add the onion. Cook gently for 10 minutes until soft and golden but not browned. Pour in the wine and boil hard until reduced and almost disappeared. Stir in the rice and coat with the butter and wine. Add a ladle of stock and the saffron and simmer, stirring until absorbed. Continue adding the stock, ladle by ladle, until all the stock has been absorbed. The rice should be very tender, thick and golden. (This should take about 20 minutes.)

Taste and season well with salt and pepper and stir in the Parmesan. Lightly whisk the egg and beat into the risotto. Spread out on a plate and let cool completely, about 1 hour. Take 1 tablespoon cold risotto and, with damp hands, spread out in the palm of one hand. Mound a small teaspoon of meat ragù in the centre. Take another tablespoon of risotto and set over the ragù to enclose it completely. Carefully roll and smooth in your hands to form a perfect round ball (or form into a cone shape with a rounded end). Continue until all the risotto and filling has been used.

To make the coating, put the flour on a plate, the beaten egg in a shallow dish and the breadcrumbs in a shallow bowl. Roll the arancine first in the flour, then in the egg and finally roll in the breadcrumbs until evenly coated. At this stage, they can be covered and left in the refrigerator for up to 1 day.

Heat the oil in a deep-fryer or wok until a crumb will sizzle immediately – 180°C (350°F). Fry a few arancine at a time for 3–5 minutes until deep golden. Drain on kitchen paper, sprinkle with salt and serve immediately (or keep warm in a low oven for up to 15 minutes).

Note For vegetarians, instead of the meat ragù filling, use 100 g finely chopped mozzarella, 4 sun-dried tomatoes in oil, drained and finely chopped, and a few finely chopped fresh basil leaves.

This is my version of Sweet Risotto Cake (*torta di riso dolce*), so popular throughout Italy. The cooked rice is often mixed with candied fruits and nuts, but this is not to everyone's taste, so I mix in amarena cherries (a great favourite of mine), ground almonds and pistachios. Normally this is cooked in a 25 cm cake tin and tends to be a bit dry, so I cook them individually and serve with amarena syrup poured over the top. Amarena cherries are available in pretty blue and white glass jars or in less expensive cans.

cherry and almond risotto puddings

budini di riso con amarene e mandorle

175 g risotto rice, preferably vialone nano

1 litre whole milk

2 tablespoons semolina

400 g canned amarena cherries, plus extra to serve

6 eggs

150 g caster sugar

50 g ground almonds

grated zest of 1 unwaxed lemon

3 tablespoons maraschino liqueur or brandy

50 g pistachio nuts, halved

6–8 ramekins, pudding or dariole moulds, lightly buttered, then dusted with semolina

a baking tray

Serves 6–8

Put the rice and the milk in a saucepan. Slowly bring to the boil, turn down the heat and simmer for 15 minutes. Drain the cherries and reserve the syrup. Halve the cherries, rinse and dry on kitchen paper.

Put the eggs, sugar, ground almonds, lemon zest and liqueur in a large bowl and beat until pale and creamy. Fold into the rice, then fold in the halved cherries and pistachios. Spoon into the moulds and level the tops. Set the filled moulds on the baking tray and bake in a preheated oven at 180°C (350°F) Gas 4 for about 25 minutes or until a wooden skewer inserted in the centre comes out clean. The puddings should be set and golden brown.

Let cool in the moulds for 5 minutes, then run a knife around the edge to loosen. Invert onto serving plates. Serve warm or cold with the reserved cherry syrup and extra cherries.

Note If you have the time, grind your own almonds and the result will be so much better. Put them in the freezer for 30 minutes, then grind them in a food processor using the pulse button. This will prevent them becoming oily.

A delicious creamy risotto based on an ancient recipe from the north-east coast of Sicily. Chocolate arrived in Sicily from the New World via the court of Spain. The Spanish used it as a drink and a flavouring ingredient. It is still made in Modica today and is slightly grainy and not over-processed, retaining its ancient roots. It is variously flavoured with vanilla, cinnamon and chilli (a flavour beloved by Sicilians). A pinch of ground chilli in the pudding adds a warmth and mysterious flavour – for adults only.

dark chocolate risotto

riso nero

3 tablespoons unsweetened cocoa powder
100 g sugar
¼ teaspoon ground cinnamon
900 ml whole milk
150 g risotto rice, preferably vialone nano
3 long strips of orange zest
100 g bitter chocolate, grated
75 g chopped candied orange peel (optional)

to serve
cinnamon sticks
candied orange peel
icing sugar
pouring cream

Serves 4

Put the cocoa, sugar and cinnamon in a small bowl and add 4 tablespoons of the milk. Mix until well blended, then add another 4 tablespoons milk.

Put the rice in a medium saucepan and stir in the cocoa-flavoured milk, the remaining milk and the strips of orange zest. Slowly bring to the boil, then reduce the heat, cover and barely simmer for 20 minutes. The rice should be very tender, creamy and slightly sloppy (if not, add a little extra hot milk). Remove the strips of orange zest and stir in the chocolate until it has completely melted, then the candied orange peel, if using.

Spoon into 4 small warm bowls or glass heatproof dishes and set a cinnamon stick and a slice of candied peel in each one. Sprinkle with icing sugar, serve immediately with pouring cream and eat while still warm.

Sounds mad, but this is a delicate, creamy vanilla ice cream, with an interesting granular texture. I love it. Its origins seem to be in Moorish Sicily, where rosewater, cinnamon and even ginger were used as flavourings. It has now become popular all over Italy. Tiny, wild strawberries, cherries cooked in red wine, fresh peaches marinated in sweet wine, or warm roasted figs – all go perfectly with this ice cream. It is ambrosial served with a spoonful of rose petal jam.

rice ice cream
gelato di riso

125 g Italian arborio rice

600 ml whole milk

1 vanilla pod, split

175 g caster sugar

600 ml double cream, chilled
(or 250 g mascarpone cheese
mixed with 300 ml milk until smooth)

1 tablespoon orange flower water or rosewater

greaseproof paper or clingfilm

an electric ice cream maker

Serves 8

Put the rice in a flameproof casserole with the milk and vanilla pod. Bring to the boil, cover tightly and bake in a preheated oven at 180°C (350°F) Gas 4 for about 1 hour until very tender. (Alternatively, simmer on top of the stove for 30 minutes until tender.) When cooked, discard the vanilla pod (rinsing and drying it to put in a jar of sugar later), stir in the sugar and cover the surface with greaseproof paper or clingfilm.

Let cool, then chill in the refrigerator for at least 1 hour. When cold, stir in the cream (or mascarpone and milk) and orange flower water or rosewater. Freeze in an ice cream maker according to the manufacturer's instructions until it is the consistency of whipped cream, then transfer to a freezer-proof container and keep in the freezer for at least 2 hours. Transfer the ice cream to the refrigerator 1 hour before serving, to soften. Serve in soft scoops, with peaches, figs or cherries.

Notes

If you do not have an ice cream machine, freeze the mixture in a freezer-proof container, whisking periodically during freezing to break down the ice crystals and ensure a smooth-textured result.

If making double quantity, 900 ml cream is enough.

websites and mail order

GROW YOUR OWN

www.seedsofitaly.sagenet.co.uk
Real Italian seeds supplied mail order for growing your own Italian fruit, vegetables and herbs.

KITCHEN EQUIPMENT

Bartolini
Via dei Servi 30/r,
Santissima Annunziata, Florence, Italy
Italian cookware shop – temple of gastronomy.

The Cooks' Kitchen
Tel: (+44) 0117 9070903 Monday to Friday,
10.00 am to 6.00 pm for catalogue.
www.thecookskitchen.com
Mail order company with everything you could need for cooking Italian-style – you can browse by country – they even have giant pepper mills.

www.cucinadirect.com
Good mail order kitchenware shop.

Divertimenti
139–141 Fulham Road,
London SW3 6SD
Tel: 020 7581 8065
Fax: 020 7823 9429

and

33–34 Marylebone High Street,
London W1U 4PT
Tel: 020 7935 0689
www.divertimenti.co.uk
Two London shops plus mail order. Knife sharpening and copper retinning service.

Lakeland Limited
Alexandra Buildings, Windermere,
Cumbria LA23 1BQ
Tel: 015394 88100
Fax: 015394 88300
www.lakelandlimited.com
Huge range of bakeware and cookery equipment available by mail order, online and from their shops. Phone for a catalogue.

ITALIAN FOOD

Baroni
Mercato Centrale, Florence, Italy
www.baronialimentari.it
The Baroni family offers top-quality condiments, oils, aged balsamic vinagars, fresh alpine butter, fresh black and white truffles in season and truffle products and will ship all over the world. Visit when in Florence, or visit the site to be transported.

Carluccio's
Tel: 020 7240 1487
www.carluccios.com
Quality Italian produce, cured goods, pasta, grain, condiments.

Esperya S.p.A.
www.esperya.com
Genuine, high-quality foods from all regions of Italy (olive oil, wine, honey, pasta, rice, puddings, charcuterie, cheeses, preserves, seafood). UK and US sites.

Fratelli Camisa
53 Charlotte Street,
London W1
www.camisa.co.uk
Camisa Direct is the mail order arm of the famous Italian deli in London, with an incredible array of food, books and hard-to-find kitchen equipment.

www.gamberorosso.it
Fascinating Italian gastronomic website (English version under construction) – books, food, wine.

www.italianmade.com
The Italian Trade Commission,
33 E 67th Street, New York, NY 10021
The US official site of the foods and wines of Italy. Includes how to eat Italian-style, history and lore of Italian foods and wines.

www.italianwinereview.com
Interesting and impartial news and information about Italian wines.

www.menu2menu.com/italglossary.html
Helpful glossary of Italian menu and cooking terms.

www.mycologue.co.uk
40 Swains Lane,
London N6 6QR
Tel: 020 7485 7063
Fax: 020 7284 4058
The internet mushroom shop. A unique selection of products to delight everyone interested in collecting, eating, cultivating or just appreciating mushrooms. Based in England, but will mail most products abroad.

The Oil Merchant Ltd
47 Ashchurch Grove,
London W12 9BU
Tel: 020 8740 1335
Fax: 020 8740 1319
E-mail the_oil_merchant@compuserve.com
Olive oil and dressings, oil, sauces, pasta, vinegar. Mail order, retail, wholesale.

Olives Direct
8/9 Williams Industrial Park,
New Milton, Hampshire BH25 6SH
Tel: 01425 613000
Fax: 01425 611636
www.olivesdirect.co.uk
Selection of the finest quality fresh olives. Nearly 30 varieties available online, as well as sun-dried tomatoes. Delivers in the UK.

Savoria Ltd
229 Linen Hall, 162–168 Regent Street,
London W1B 5TB
Tel: 0870 2421823
Fax: 0870 2421823
www.savoria.co.uk
Savoria is a mail order company that sells i veri sapori d'Italia, the true tastes of Italy. Food created by Italian artisans – hidden gems from all regions of Italy, including the islands.

Valvona & Crolla
19 Elm Row,
Edinburgh EH7 4AA
Tel: 0131 556 6066
www.valvonacrolla.co.uk
Italian deli products, particularly cured foods, oils, wines and condiments.

index